DR. ERICA MILLER

THANKS
FOR MY
JOURNEY

A HOLOCAUST SURVIVOR'S STORY
of LIVING FEARLESSLY

EMERALD BOOK CO.

Published by Emerald Book Company
Austin, TX
www.emeraldbookcompany.com

Distributed by Emerald Book Company

For ordering information or special discounts for bulk purchases, please contact Emerald Book Company at PO Box 91869, Austin, TX 78709, 512.891.6100.

Design and composition by Greenleaf Book Group LLC
Cover design by Greenleaf Book Group LLC

Publisher's Cataloging-In-Publication Data
(Prepared by The Donohue Group, Inc.)
Miller, Erica, 1933-
    Thanks for my journey : a holocaust survivor's story of living fearlessly / Erica Miller. -- 2nd ed.
    p. : ill. ; cm.
    First ed.: The Dr. Erica Miller story : from trauma to triumph. Nashville, Tenn. : Cold River Studio, c2009.
    Includes bibliographical references.
    ISBN: 978-1-937110-26-0
    1. Miller, Erica, 1933- 2. Jews--Romania--Biography. 3. Clinical psychologists--United States--Biography. 4. Businesswomen--United States--Biography. 5. Holocaust survivors--United States--Biography. I. Title. II. Title: Dr. Erica Miller story.
DR266.3 .M55 2012
949.8/02/092   2011945835

Part of the Tree Neutral® program, which offsets the number of trees consumed in the production and printing of this book by taking proactive steps, such as planting trees in direct proportion to the number of trees used: www.treeneutral.com

Printed in the United States of America on acid-free paper

11 12 13 14 15 16 10 9 8 7 6 5 4 3 2 1

Second Edition

DEDICATION

To my lifelong partner, Jerry, who lent a big hand by staying out of the way so that I could evolve and have it all.

To my children, Diana and Johnny, my biggest fans and most candid critics, who survived and prospered because of me and in spite of me.

And last but not least, to my grandchildren, the icing on the cake of life, who will know me someday and ponder.

CONTENTS

ACKNOWLEDGMENTS

I always knew that someday I would document my life, my incredible journey, for my children and grandchildren. "Someday" perhaps never would have come were it not for Doris Lora of Life Journey Editions, a former colleague of mine, who knocked on my door one day and offered to assist me in telling my story. She took down and organized hours upon hours of taped interviews, and provided structure and order for the web of my life.

It was an exciting process, to say the least. I told my children that parts of my life story are juicy—about my virginity and so forth. "Oh boy, I'm not sure I want to hear it all," my son commented.

I wish to thank my husband, Jerry, and my children, Diana and Johnny, for their contributions. Their candor is a compliment.

I wish to thank my sister, Judith, for her Shoah interview segment and for remembering details about our family that I had buried or forgotten.

I would be remiss if I were not to give special credit to my daughter, Diana, who spent many hours by my side so that I could bounce off her any and all changes to the original text of this book.

Her input and contributions shine all through the text. Exploring the pages of my life was a special journey for both of us.

I thank Laura Gallop and Sophia Fischer for their editing touches, and last but not least, I thank Gerri Knilans from Trade Press Services for her steadfast guidance in getting this book published.

This is a memoir told through my eyes. This is my life story as I see it, and I take full responsibility for the contents. My intention has been to be candid, tempered by consideration. I apologize if I have said anything hurtful.

STAGE OF LIFE RECEPTION, 1991

PROLOGUE

5:30 a.m., December 30, 2005

I jump out of bed, not sure if I am awake or in a nightmare. My senses are overwhelmed—explosions, thick smoke, the rattling of fire raging mercilessly and engulfing my universe. In an instant I'm back in the war zone of my youth, reliving the ferocity of explosions, fire, bombs, and smoke. Although I am half asleep, my thoughts come quickly: "Run, run for your life. Get out." I feel panic, like a trapped animal looking to escape to survive. My breathing is shallow. My heart is beating fast.

I am jolted back into the present. I look over to the bed. Jerry does not move. The mayhem failed to arouse him. I am fully awake now. It is not the war of my youth. Our home is engulfed in flames; there is no time to waste. I try to open the bedroom door facing the hallway. There is no passage. The fire is raging toward the bedroom, the last room to fall prey to the unleashed hungry monster of nature. I slam the door closed.

"Jerry, wake up! Wake up; we have to get out of here. Hurry."
It seems it takes him forever to get out of our king-size bed. He looks bewildered, clumsy, searching for his shirt and slippers. He is so slow! "Jerry, there is no time! Hurry, hurry up, let's get out of here!"

I run through the back door of our bedroom and into the garden. I am out! I see the spectacular fireworks raging mercilessly through the entire length of our beautiful ranch house. I look back. Jerry is not behind me. I turn back and run inside, literally dragging him out. He's still sleepy, unaware of the danger.

As we exit, the roof over our bedroom collapses, charring our massive bed to ashes. Later, the fire marshal says that had we not run out when we did, had we been in deep sleep in the middle of the night, we would have burned to death. Just like in the crematorium I had avoided as a child in the concentration camp.

Barefoot and half naked, we stumble toward the front of the house, where our neighbors, awakened by the terrible sounds of a home being consumed by fire, try to comfort us, offering shelter, shoes, blankets, and coffee. It is early in the morning and cold, very cold.

I stand in front of the house, watching, mesmerized, as the fire envelops our entire beautiful home and its precious contents, collected over a lifetime, and turning it all into debris in minutes.

Similar to people's reports of near-death experiences, I see all my furniture, dishes, pictures, and other treasured memorabilia pass before my eyes, succumbing to the fierce force of the devastation. I can do nothing. I'm immobilized, helpless.

All I can do is stand silent, a witness to the inferno.

Suddenly, the survivor in me kicks in. It is not I who is burning. Jerry and I are safe, truly safe. These are things that are burning, just things. "Things, things" is the refrain of the song of my thoughts. The Nazis did not get me then; the fire did not get me now.

To think that fate has it that twice in my life, I almost burned to death! I can see newspaper headlines: "Spared by Nazis, She Avoided Gas Chambers Only to Burn to Death in Own Home."

I am so lucky to have the gift of life a bit longer. We are alive. That's all that matters. Remember, things are just things. You enter the world naked and exit the world in kind. I Am Alive!

It's all about fate, destiny, or beshert (the Yiddish word I like to use). I was meant to survive once more, saved from the rage of burning hell. I shall continue celebrating life, and I will spread optimism and goodwill in my world until I die. I have this vision: I close my eyes, and in the embrace of my family—children and grandchildren—I peacefully cross the threshold, ready to join the universe and its mysterious splendor. "Thanks for my journey," I am smiling. I feel peaceful. I feel safe. I am transcending above and beyond toward my eternal journey. "Poof" goes my soul to never-never land.

PART I

RUMANIA, 1933–1949

A TRAGICALLY BRIEF CHILDHOOD

German is my mother tongue, and Rumania is my birthplace, but I had to leave both behind quite early in life.

I was born on November 10, 1933, in Tshernovitz, Bukovina, a province in Rumania. The area had been part of Austria when my parents were young; hence my mother tongue was German. Later it became Rumania, then Moldavia, and now it is part of Ukraine. I had one sister, Judith, or Dita, as we called her. She was four and a half years older than I.

My father, Emmanuel Gelber (Mendy), son of Eta and Julius Gelber, was a tall, handsome man, popular with the ladies. He was smart, well read, and artistic. He cut quite a figure strolling down the Morgenbessergasse, the narrow street leading to our home. My mother's older brother, Oskar, said to my father one day, "Mendel, you are going to marry my sister, Fani. She's a virgin and you'll get a big trousseau." So Mendel married Fani Turkfeld, a rich girl who was smart but uneducated. It was time for her to marry. She was already pushing twenty, which was considered old for marriage at that time.

According to my mother, the marriage was a good one for a few years, until my father started to fool around. According to my father, my mother had a vivid imagination and the marriage was fine. What I think and what I know is that they were mismatched but did the best they could. By my standards, they had a loveless, yet functional, relationship.

We had family dinners, holidays, and vacations together. As a child, I never witnessed abuse or disrespect between my parents. They took care of each other and us. We were a family!

FAMILY

Three of my grandparents died before I was born. The only one I knew was my father's mother, Eta Gelber, and by the time I was born, she was deaf and blind and in her eighties. When we visited her on Sundays, she was invariably lying in bed, gray and nearly immobile with vacant milky eyes and a musty smell from aging organs. She would reach out and touch me to "see" who was there. To say I hated those weekly visits is an understatement. She died when I was about four years old.

My father's father, Julius Gelber, was a teacher, which was unusual at that time. Most people were uneducated, and many were merchants. It was prestigious to be a teacher. I don't know exactly what he taught—probably the Talmud or some other Jewish subject. The family had no money but combined a deep love for learning with a persistent motivation to get ahead. My determination to attain an education, my intense interest in seeking knowledge and academia must have come through my father's side.

My mother's parents, Yetta and Samuel Turkfeld, were uneducated, yet they made a good living from their owner-operated steel factory. Owning your own business, especially in a line of blue-collar work, was unheard of for Jews of that era. My aptitude and interest in seeking out entrepreneurial business ventures definitely were transmitted to me from my mother's genetic pool of traits.

I view the legacy of my forty-six chromosomes as precious ancestral treasures gifted to me, only me, and no other. What a humbling thought it is to be uniquely woven in as part of a never-ending chain of links to my past and future.

The family steel business was on the first floor, and my aunts, uncles, cousins, and our family lived on the second. I remember sneaking into the work area of the factory (as children we were prohibited from going there) and walking down the narrow aisle. I could hear the grind of the welding and see the sparks flying as the steel was being foundered. I dared to disobey. My curiosity superseded the potential consequences. I liked the rush and excitement I felt pushing through the doors close to me. Warnings and punishments by my elders failed to rein in my adventurous nature. I walked to the beat of my own drums. I still do.

My grandfather, Sam, ran the factory with three of his sons, and my grandmother, Yetta, was doing what women were supposed to do: remain barefoot and pregnant in the kitchen, cooking and cleaning.

My grandmother was a short, skinny, hardworking, serious woman. She never smiled. I assume she did not have a muscle to spare. She was probably overworked and underappreciated. Twelve kids and a husband—can you imagine that? I can't.

Among her many children, Yetta's firstborn daughter, Gusta, married young and moved to South America, leaving Fani (my mother), the only other girl, to help Yetta care for the men and the household.

When my mother was born, there was little room for her in the house, so they put her cradle under the table. In many ways, Fani never completely got out from under the narrow and limited space of her lifelong existence. She was always just an extension of everyone else.

Fani was allowed to attend school just on Saturdays, since she was the only girl left to help her mother with chores. Week in, week out, every Saturday, dressed in her one and only dress, Fani went to school with trepidation. The kids would point a finger at her and laugh, "It must be Saturday. Here comes Fani, always wearing the same dress."

In spite of the humiliation and mockery from her peers, Fani feasted off the crumbs of education as best she could. Throughout her life, she remained hungry for knowledge and embarrassed by her scribbled handwriting and her limited literacy.

Unfortunately for her, she was a prisoner of her times. She never evolved. She was not able to push the envelope, whereas I was able to break through and go beyond the traditional narrow-mindedness of gender limitation.

"Are you proud of me, Mama? I did what you couldn't do for both of us!"

"Don't tell me that because I'm a girl, I cannot climb a tree or swim in the sea like the boys do. Don't tell me that because I'm a woman I cannot have a family and a thriving career as well. Don't tell me to rein in my adventurous nature because I'm a woman.

"Mama, do you hear me? Are you proud of me?"

Praise from my mother, no matter how hard I tried and how much I deserved it, would never reach my hungry ears. Yet, I know she loved me; she loved me very much. I did not know it then, but I knew it later.

My mother never received affection from her mother, who perhaps was just too busy to show any. In turn, my mother was not demonstrative at all to her husband or daughters. I used to beg my mother for affection. "Mama, please give me a kiss. Give me a hug." But she'd shoo me away, saying she was busy. I would persist, "Mama, did I do anything wrong?" She'd turn away: "No, no, go away." She was not a person of many words. She was shy and inhibited.

On the other hand, Papa was affectionate. He was also emotional and had a temper, a trait I share. But when an outburst was over, it was over. He did not carry a grudge. I wish I could say the same about my mother. She was weighted down by a deep barrel of grudges that never saw the light of day. Her silence spoke volumes.

My father was a self-proclaimed artist and poet. As far back as I remember, he always doodled. I have some of his paintings proudly displayed in my home. He used to write poetry as well. He was often the life of the party; everybody liked him. He was articulate, handsome, and always immaculately dressed. My mother, on the other hand, though good-looking, paid little attention to her appearance and grooming. In addition to her quietness, she barely spoke the language of the land—whether Rumanian, Hebrew, or English. She spoke only German. She expressed herself through her children. I was always proud of my father and embarrassed by my mother.

In retrospect, I can see that my father was a flawed person and my mother was a model of kindness, loyalty, and devotion to her family. My strong attachment to my children mimics hers. However, unlike my mother and luckily for my children, although I love being with them, I have a full and exciting life apart from them as well.

Early in their marriage, Papa was attentive to Mama. He shared his day at work and read newspapers to her to keep her informed. When Papa got tired of the one-sided communication and stopped sharing his life with her, she felt abandoned and very lonely.

SAMUEL TURKFELD

YETTA TURKFELD

MY MOTHER, FANI TURKFELD

MY FATHER,
MENDY GELBER

MY MOTHER, FANI
TURKFELD GELBER

OUR COMPOUND
(HOUSE/FACTORY) IN
TSHERNOVITZ,
ROMANIA, WHERE I
SPENT MY FIRST 7 YEARS

MY FATHER AND ME

MY FAMILY, ABOUT 1937, L TO R: JUDITH (DITA), MY FATHER
EMMANUEL (MENDY) GELBER, MYSELF (AGE 4), MY MOTHER
FANI TURKFELD GELBER

Eventually, the marriage deteriorated. Papa kept growing, and she stayed under the table, just as her cradle had been when she was an infant. She would watch his every move and accuse him of straying. He couldn't go out and buy a pack of cigarettes without her following him. The honeymoon was definitely over.

EARLIEST MEMORIES

I was seven years old when my world as I knew it fell apart. It was 1941. German soldiers were everywhere. Something scary was going on, but I did not know what. My memories from before that point are scant—bits and pieces here and there.

The trauma of my war experiences impaired my memory of events not only before but also during and in the years after that horrific time. Some of my recollections from before the war were that of a good life. We used to get dressed up and go for a walk on the Herrengasse (a famous street in Tshernovitz) to the park every Sunday—Papa, Mama, Dita, and I. We have a photo of us strolling along the "gasse." I vaguely remember going to the beach on the Prut River and having fun. The factory building, which was my home during my early childhood in the late 1930s, was like a compound. Each of the Turkfeld siblings and their families had a one-bedroom apartment on the second floor of the factory. There was a kitchen/sitting room and the bedroom that my parents shared with my sister and me.

Among all my extended family who shared our home, my most memorable and favorite aunt was Aunt Olga, who was always baking cookies. Uncle Oskar brought her home from his travels during World War I. She was born Christian. She had left her family behind, embraced Judaism, and became a devout Jew. She scrupulously observed all the dietary laws and prepared all the holiday meals for the whole Turkfeld clan. Unimaginably and unforgivably, she was referred to as the "Goya" (a term that can be used derogatorily for a non-Jewish individual) by some members of our family until the end of her gracious life. Prejudice is, and will always remain, an incurable disease of the feeble-minded.

My five cousins who lived in our compound were an important part of my early life. We had such fun playing games in the backyard. A beautiful lilac tree grew there. Those were happy times, and I loved that tree. I grow lilac bushes in my own yard in Southern California, and to this day, their sweet scent takes me right back to that idyllic time before the war when I would play with my cousins. Even though my lilacs are not as fragrant as the tree I remember, they are still beautiful and cherished.

My sister had an issue with food. She was chubby, and our mother would hide food from her. I, on the other hand, was very skinny, and my mother would try to feed me like a goose. She used to hold me down, pinch my nose closed, and push food into my throat like they did with geese to fatten them up for the holidays. I would rebel, struggling against her and shouting, "Don't make me!" She would ignore me and continue to push food into my throat. The way I got even and fought back was by being contrary, ignoring her, and misbehaving at any opportunity I had, and there were many.

My mother couldn't get by with spanking me because I learned to hold my breath until I turned blue. Instead, she pinched me. It really hurt, but I was not about to cry! I showed her!

Only once do I remember my father hitting me on the behind, although I don't remember exactly what I did. I had a big mouth and probably said something I shouldn't have. When my father scolded me, I taunted him, "Go ahead. Hit me all you want. I won't cry." He continued to hit me— I had black and blue bruises for some time—but I waited until he left the room and then I cried in private. I'm still like that. When there's a trauma, I do whatever has to be done, detached and purposeful. Then, after the crisis is over, I allow myself to be vulnerable, shake some, and move on.

My mother was fair-skinned and blond, as were my sister and all of my cousins. My complexion was dark, like my father's. There were a lot of Gypsies in Rumania. People used to tease me that I did not really belong to my family, that I fell off a Gypsy wagon, and my parents picked me up and took me in. They called me Zigeunerin, Gypsy girl.

I always felt different. There was no one who looked like me in the family. I still feel unconnected and separate—walking to the beat of my own drummer, with or without the approval of those close to me.

Dita recalls that our mother used to take her for strolls through the neighborhood but would leave me behind with the maid because I was ugly. I always wanted to be told that I was pretty. Although I don't remember my mother's words, I understood that my sister was the pretty one and I was the smart but unattractive one. As a child and adolescent, it seemed to me that rather than rely on my looks, I would have to prove myself through education—and I did. But first, I had to survive a war.

NAZI HORRORS

"I believed I could not survive this, and I indeed survived, but do not ask me how." —An unknown German poet, quoted in Papa's journal

TO THE CATTLE CARS

By the time I was six, the political situation in Bukovina had deteriorated into chaos. Rumania had signed a trade agreement with Germany in 1939, followed by several more treaties that placed Rumania under heavy Third Reich influence. Germany ceded parts of Bukovina to the Soviet Union and Bulgaria. Rumania was declared a "National Legionary State," and democracy essentially disappeared. In that chaos, the right-wing Iron Guard tried to seize power but was defeated. By 1940, Germany had gained more and more influence, and a special intelligence unit began to suppress all dissent. That was the beginning of a policy of persecution and extermination of Jews.

Being hunted like animals is an indelible memory for me. The systematic deportation and extermination of Jews had begun. We were not spared! One day, the Germans came to our factory unannounced as part of their relentless search in pursuit of prey. I distinctly remember Papa and Mama hurrying us up to the attic of the factory.

There were many of us crammed into the small space of the attic, all huddled together in the dark on the prickly hay. We heard the German soldiers with their menacing, barking dogs coming up the stairs, closer and closer. My father's breathing sounded loud and heavy. I sensed his panic. My mother put her hand over my mouth so I would not scream. I was so frightened. I couldn't breathe. My parents knew that if we were found, we would be beaten, herded together, forced into boxcars on the train, or shot.

Much later in my life, here in Los Angeles, a friend who was studying to be a cosmetologist suggested giving me a facial. She put a mud mask on my face, and suddenly I felt constricted, out of control. I had a flashback to the attic and my mother's hand over my mouth. I tried to calm myself: "You are not a child; you are not in danger; you are safe; you are OK." But to my consternation, I couldn't calm myself. I started to panic. I began to hyperventilate. I called to my friend, "Eva, Eva, get this mask off of me. Get it off me!" Quickly she washed it off. Amazing! My adult reassuring thoughts and cognitive abilities did not hold up in the face of my traumatic flashback.

Whenever we were given a heads-up that the Germans were coming, we repeated the same hiding routine. It happened numerous times. I did not understand what was happening—the grim faces and whispers, "Germans, Jewish . . ." We are Jewish. We have to hide. No one tells me what is going on.

"Mama, why do we have to hide again? Mama, Mama!"

"Stop it, Erica, stop with the questions," she said.

"But Mama, I don't want to be Jewish, Jewish, Jewish, Jewish, Mama!"

"For the last time, stop it," she repeated.

"Papa, Papa!" There was no explanation from him either. He did not hear me. He looked through me. I was invisible. I had never seen him like this before. The stress was getting to him. He was falling to pieces in front of my eyes. He could not handle the anxiety of wondering and waiting. He felt humiliated having to crouch in corners like a hunted animal.

He finally declared, "I cannot tolerate this any longer. We will go voluntarily to the trains rather than hide and wait to be captured." He was either completely nuts or incredibly courageous. I can only imagine how difficult it had to be for him to make that decision.

From Papa's Journal:

Because I worked for the Russians from May 1940 to July 1941, I was put on the "blacklist." A former Christian colleague and friend warned me to quickly disappear. Hearing that the Gestapo was after me, I

*decided that being deported was the safer way to go. If
we continued to hide, it was only a matter of time.*

Thanks to the steel factory's output of product for the war machine, my mother's brothers and their families had permission from the Germans to stay in Tshernovitz. They were lucky they stayed behind and survived. My father's family, on the other hand, suffered a different fate. His brother and his brother's family were deported and perished in the camps. I don't know where they were sent. His sister married a Christian, moved to Argentina, and completely cut off ties to the family. My father wrote to her after the war, but she refused to respond. I think she suffered from a variation of Stockholm syndrome.

Once the decision was made to leave, my father found a Rumanian neighbor with a horse and buggy who, for a fee, took us to the cattle cars. We had to leave everything behind except for small bundles of clothes.

As we made our way to the trains, crowds of people swarmed around us as if in a daze, carrying pitifully small packages of belongings just like we were. We were forced to leave behind cherished mementos of a lifetime. We each wore two or three sets of clothing, layer upon layer, in a desperate hope to salvage a few things and have some protection from the elements. It was wintertime. We looked funny, all puffed up like gigantic stuffed puppets, unrecognizable. My father, my tall, handsome father, looked so odd, with his overstuffed arms and chest covered with two shirts, suits, a jacket, and a coat. All of us and those around us wore the required yellow Star of David, which marked us as refuse to get rid of.

At the train station, people were screaming, struggling to stay together, and fearful of getting lost. Mother held on to Dita and me for dear life. People were moaning and crying, clinging to each other, and hanging on to their children. Some people lost their loved ones, and there was much screaming as they desperately sought each other out among the stream of refugees.

At the train station, we were pushed onto a cattle car. Papa, Mama, Dita, and I held to one another tightly as we were herded toward the back of the freight car and forced onto the floor. The train was filled to capacity with people. I could hardly breathe. I pushed closer to my mother. People were pushing against each other, too close for comfort, way too close. The train made many stops on the way to the unknown. The steel doors slid open, and in came fresh air and fresh terror.

From Dita's Journal:

Soldiers with guns would drag out the men and begin
hitting them with bayonets. I will never forget my
father lying in the filthy mud, holding his arms over his
face, trying to shield himself from the senseless blows,
the "joy" beatings, as we came to call them.

From Papa's Journal:

*Like cattle, we were beaten with no mercy and driven
out of the train. We were thrown to the ground as the
perpetrators yelled, "Filthy Jews."*

I crouched deep into the corner of the cattle car. Mama was
nearly smothering me with her body. I thought, "It's a good thing
we are in the back. Maybe they won't get to us and beat us." Then
the train whistle would blow, and the soldiers would jump off the
train. We would not see more until the next stop and another
wave of terror. I further remember singing silently to myself, "schmutzige Juden, schmutzige Juden" ("filthy Jews, filthy Jews") over
and over again in perfect harmony with the steady, repetitive beat
of the train tracks—tum tatum . . . tatum, filthy Jews . . . filthy Jews
. . . filthy Jews . . . tatum . . . tatum . . . tatum. At least for a moment
I forgot where I was—but just for a moment.

We were sitting on the floor of the cattle car, on top of each
other, with barely room to move. This experience created for me
a deep-seated case of claustrophobia, which never left me. I crave
privacy and must always have my own space. Don't stand too close
to me. Don't intrude on my space. Don't go through my drawers.
Don't look in my purse. Don't help yourself to my things. It could
not have been easy for my husband and children to understand or
comply with my need for privacy.

I don't know how many days we spent in the cattle cars. From Rumania to Ukraine, where we were being taken, is quite a distance. It could have been days or weeks. We made stops to pick up other disheveled refugees. I can still hear the sobbing and wailing inside and outside the train. There was no food, no water, no toilets. We didn't know anyone else on the train with us, and we couldn't see their faces. They were just faceless strangers sharing the same destiny, being herded away into the unknown, into the abyss.

THE CAMP

After what seemed like endless, trying days, the train arrived at the dreaded destination. The detention camp was located in Mogilev, in the province of Transnistria in Ukraine. The doors slid open. "Out, out, you filthy Jews!" the guards shouted. Icy rain poured down. There was a sea of mud everywhere. People got separated, lost, and one could hear names being called out everywhere. "Rifka? Yettel? Jacob? Leo?"

My mother hung on to my arm tightly, something she continued to do all through her life. I hated it. Even when I was an adult, out on my own, she would hang on to me and call me late at night to make sure I had gotten home safely. I was annoyed with her and wished she would stop needing to know my every move. Looking back, I wish I could have been kinder. She was afraid to lose me. She just wanted to know I was safe.

Once off the trains, we walked and walked to reach the camp. We were covered with layers of mud. We were freezing, wet, filthy, miserable, and terrified. We must have walked a long time, because my shoes had holes and the cold mud just seeped through. Under the cover of darkness, Papa stopped at a peasant's house and asked for water. They closed the door in our faces. The yellow Star of David was the mark of death.

The next day we arrived at a mountain. There were Rumanian and German soldiers everywhere, guarding the Rumanian-German camp. Just over the mountain, beyond where we could see, was our camp, or so we heard. An eerie silence descended upon the frightened crowd, upon me. Yes, I was frightened. I could not see or hear a thing but my heart beating and my stomach growling. The silence surrounding my universe was deafening, but not for long. The familiar shouting voices of the guards became louder and louder until they were right on top of me, behind me, in front of me, everywhere. Then, suddenly, the soldiers grabbed my father and viciously beat him for no apparent reason. "Why? Why are they beating Papa? What did he do?" There were no answers. I remember looking upon my father's attackers and being immobilized, helpless. There was nothing I could do to help Papa. No child should bear witness to such a degradation of one's parent. It was fortunate that he was wearing layers upon layers of clothes, which prevented serious injury.

Later in life, as a mental health professional, I was able to inspire, empower, and coach the oppressed in their plight against abuse and brutality in their lives. Time and time again, I was able to right the wrong done to my father.

In order to get over the mountain, we had to wade through mud and debris. It was slippery, and people kept sliding back down the path, unable to make it to the top.

In exchange for jewelry, the soldiers with their long sticks assisted the refugees in getting to our destination. Without pause, the women took off rings and necklaces and handed them over to their tormentors. My mother, though, saved one of her wedding rings by hiding it, probably in her bra. She gave the soldiers the rest of the jewelry she had so the four of us could be helped over the hill. When I think back, I realize that my mother was a tough, brave soul whenever she needed to be. I think I emulated her in that as well.

Night had fallen and it was pitch black. Throughout our desperate ranks, a rumor began circulating that some people were being taken to a place from which no one came out alive. The "good place" to reach was the camp in Mogilev. At this news, my father made a risky decision. Quietly, my parents, sister, and I crept out of the ranks, bolted into the darkness, and crawled toward a dim light in the distance. We came upon a peasant's cottage and knocked on the door. The door opened, and we could see several families huddled together in one room. Papa immediately said that he had some money. The man grunted his assent and pocketed the rubles, and we found a spot of shelter for the night. Early the next morning, before daybreak, we were shaken awake and told to hurry and get out. Our host didn't want any trouble.

From Papa's Journal:

I recall the horrendous night. My thinking became confused and I started to hallucinate. The small flickering light in that room became like a fireball; I saw visions of green palms and crested clear waters. I don't know if it was seconds, minutes, or hours later that I woke up abruptly and saw the haggard faces of my wife and children, dressed in their filthy clothes, ready to move on, again into the unknown.

The memory of the mud and soaking-wet coldness stays with me to this day! Hour after hour, we trudged forward, willing our feet to take yet another step. Exhausted beyond measure, we finally got to the camp in Mogilev. I don't remember how long it took, but it was a very long time, probably days. Those who had not bolted from the ranks during the night were never heard from again. We also were spared from the terrible typhoid epidemic that had raged through Mogilev, leaving people dead in the streets. As with our ancestors in Egypt, the Angel of Death passed over us. We survived.

In Mogilev, we were shoved into a small space in a building

surrounded by barbed wire. We were kept like monkeys in a zoo. There were about fifty people—men, women, and children—in one small room. Each family huddled together in a small space. One old lady moaned and sobbed softly for what seemed like the entire time. She had become separated from her family. She had no one to lean on. I will never ever forget the wrenched, contorted features of that face.

A specific part of Mogilev was designated as a holding camp for Jews scheduled to be transferred to the gas chambers for the "final solution" as soon as possible. Certain local peasants had to vacate their properties to create housing for the refugees, whereas the local Jewish inhabitants had to take in and share their meager dwellings. Eventually we were assigned to a small house that belonged to a mother and adult daughter, who were forced to share it with us. The room was tiny, but it was a room nevertheless. I can see it clearly. There was a narrow bed, a small table with three chairs, and a bucket of water where we washed up. I do not remember what type of toilet facilities there were. Probably a hole in the backyard.

Frequently, Papa did not come home until very late. It was just my mother, my sister, and I, huddled together in that bed, wondering when the Germans would come for us. Years later I learned that my father, who spoke both German and Rumanian, worked long into the night for the Germans at their headquarters.

The window in our tiny room was a little, narrow opening, which provided me with a daily dose of dark—very dark—entertainment.

Here I was, a seven-year-old kid, standing on a box so I could look out onto the daily caravan of corpses passing beneath my window. The bodies—skeletons with dried-out skin—were piled on top of the wagon with the trash. Sometimes there would be a hand or leg hanging out, or bodies here and there thrown into the wagon like refuse. Two ghostly looking inmates pulled the wagon through the alley. Every morning I stood on the box and peered out as the infestation of death rolled by. I recall thinking, "Will I be next? Maybe tomorrow it will be my body tossed upon the wagon." I do not remember being afraid. My thoughts were matter of fact. I was detached. I still am.

MANNA FROM HEAVEN

Berta Turkfeld, my aunt, had a rich brother, Yujiu, who lived in Argentina. Somehow he heard about our plight in the camp in Mogilev. Through the black market, he managed to smuggle money to us so that we could buy some essentials from the local peasants. The way this worked out seemed to be a miracle. The story was that my mother would have dreams the night before a black market courier was supposed to arrive. His visits were irregular, so she never knew when he would come. But she would always dream about his arrival.

The morning after the dream, she would go to a certain spot along the barbed-wire fence and, sure enough, there was the person with some rubles. With this currency, Mama was able to buy some potatoes and bread. Yujiu was responsible for keeping us and several other families alive. There is no doubt in my mind that without his efforts, we would have starved to death.

I never met him, but years later my sister was in Israel when Yujiu visited there. She thanked him on behalf of our family for keeping us alive.

Occasionally, we were able to purchase eggs and cornmeal. Mama would make a treat for us—*mamaliga* (polenta). It is still one of my favorite side dishes. My mother would try to make sure we were fed first, while she would scarcely eat. I remember once that Papa, Dita, and I were standing around Mama, trying to cajole her into eating some scrambled eggs because she was so frail.

Along the barbed-wire fence was an entrance gate to the camp, guarded by a German soldier. Mama always emphasized, "Erica, you must not go near there. Keep away from the gate. Don't go near there!" But true to form, I went anyway. My curiosity was stronger than my fear. Suddenly a huge German guard spotted me and called out, "Komm her, kleines Mädel"—"Come here, little girl."

I panicked! "Now I've done it," I thought. "I didn't listen to Mama."

He looked at me carefully. "What's your name?" he asked sternly.

"Erica," I replied in a shaken voice, frozen with fear.

He reached down and stroked my hair. "At home, I have a little girl just like you," he said softly. To my amazement, tears appeared in his eyes. Then he sang me a song. I'll never forget that moment. It is as if it happened yesterday. It was so totally unexpected and confusing: a sweet song from this dreadful German Nazi to an eight-year-old Jewish child.

"Auf der Heide blumt ein kleines Blumelein Und es heisst, Erica."

("In the meadow, a little flower is blossoming, and the flower's name is Erica.")

A heartbeat later, the German's face turned stone cold, and he advised me to go back where I came from since it was not safe for a little girl to be there. I didn't share this experience with any-one. I wasn't stupid, and I was not about to get in trouble with my mother. Keeping secrets was and is easy for me. Later in life, as a therapist treating famous or infamous patients, my lips were sealed. Secrets I was entrusted with never saw the light of day. A secret is a secret, and that is that.

I remember playing outside the house in the narrow space in front of the barbed wire that surrounded the camp. We children, as bizarre and morbid as the circumstances might sound, did what children do: made up games in which we jumped over the length and width of the twisted, lifeless cadavers, making sure not to touch them, playing ball and horsing around. I also recall a little shack where we played games such as "doctor and nurse." We even put on little plays with dancing and singing. I used to have a good little voice. Everyone said I would be a stage actress someday.

My education was inconsistent and scant at best, yet we were surrounded by teachers who were refugees like us. My sister, who was older, attended makeshift schools. In addition to basics such as reading and math, she even learned French. I do not recall participating in any educational endeavors then, yet back in Rumania (after liberation), when starting fifth grade also meant entering school for the first time ever, I possessed basic reading, writing, and arithmetic skills. Someone had to have taught me how to read and write.

Looking back on those days, I often wonder: What was little Erica's frame of mind? What was I thinking? I don't know. In reflection, what I do know is that I was luckier than many other children. I was never separated from my mother. My mother's warm body next to mine, with her nonverbal message that "someday everything will be all right," eased my fears and gave me assurance and confidence. I recall being amazed as I witnessed my strong, confident father breaking down and crying on multiple occasions, whereas my mother remained a pillar of emotional strength. I never saw her cry until years later, in America, when she held my six-month-old daughter, Diana, in her arms.

I will never forget how we all suffered from jaundice. Our faces were yellow, and our eyes bulged out from their sockets. We looked like ghosts, yellow ghosts. The condition repeated itself several times while we were in camp. We could not get rid of it. To this day, I cannot donate blood because of my history of jaundice.

And then there were the lice. Living in such cramped quarters with so many people invited an army of the little bloodsuckers, which feasted endlessly on our emaciated bodies. They were everywhere, and our hair was filled with them. I still remember the noise—a little pop that would occur whenever I squeezed a louse to death between two fingernails. They have a hard shell sort of like a fish egg, and they smell! What a strong, pestlike odor a little squeezed louse has. Our lice were the "good lice." They were not the typhoid carriers. One of my favorite tasks was to be on the hunt for the little bloodsuckers. We deloused ourselves constantly and washed our hair frequently with gasoline to try to keep lice in check and keep them from multiplying. We purchased gasoline from peasants who came to the barbed wire surrounding the camp. Now, when I put gas in my car, the odor still reminds me of the little, bloodsucking lice. This is but one of many reoccurring flashbacks from those days.

Four years! I barely remember what I did during those long years. I have only a few memories of that dreadful experience. Defense mechanisms are a wonderful thing. It had to have been horrendous for me, to have to block out nearly everything and everyone, including the children I roomed with, for four years!

Four years—an eternity! From age seven to eleven. Where and how did the time go by? No memories of names or faces? Did I not get close to anyone? How could that have happened? Trauma happened.

To this day I am sorry to say that other than my family, I feel close to only a few people. All through my life, people came and left me without a feeling of loss on my part. Detachment is one of my most potent defense mechanisms—the defense against loss. My entire investment is in my family, especially my children. They know it. I hope it is not too much of a burden on them.

Ours was a success story. Papa, Mama, Dita, and I came out alive, if barely. People in our camp died waiting. They died from starvation, yellow fever, and typhoid. They dropped like flies. Inmates who had the task of picking up dead bodies could not keep up.

Later in life, I heard my parents comment that no other intact family known to them was as fortunate as we were. There does not seem to be any rhyme or reason as to who lived and who died.

Why us? Why was our life spared while others perished? Who knows? Who cares? I am so lucky to be alive. The refrain of my song of life has been and always will be, "I am so lucky to be alive."

LIBERATION: ONE DEGREE OF FREEDOM

In 1944, the war ended in Mogilev. The Germans retreated and the Russians arrived. Bombs were dropping everywhere. The noise of guns, explosions, and people screaming was deafening. The town was engulfed in smoke from faraway fires. There was mayhem everywhere, not unlike when our saga started four years earlier.

Liberation happened like this. One day there was a knock at the door of our little room, where the four of us huddled together. Standing before us were two German soldiers looking for food. They came into the room. They looked disheveled, hungry, and dirty—a far cry from the buttoned-up, arrogant, cruel Gestapo tormentors of a few weeks earlier. Nevertheless, Dita and I tried to shrink into the floor. My mother had some eggs that she handed over to them. Apparently they were hungry and desperate. They did not harm us. They were on the run. The Russians were coming!

LET MY FATHER GO!

The mother and daughter who had been forced to share their quarters with us told the arriving Russian soldiers that my father had collaborated with the Germans. Russian soldiers arrived at the door of our gloomy room, picked up my Papa, and put him in jail. In Russian jails, people were locked up first and the authorities asked questions later. Here we were, surrounded by everyone exulting in having been freed, but for us liberation brought more terror. An incredible predicament: to be freed by the Russians on one hand and incarcerated by them on the other—based on the hearsay of two disgruntled women!

Not only had my father experienced the brunt of the Nazis' torment in the camp, but also, incredibly, he was thrown into a Russian jail with criminals and murderers. The cell, we later learned, didn't have a toilet, just a hole in the corner of the same room. For weeks, he lived in unbelievable filth and degradation!

We were not about to leave without Papa. My mother may have been academically impoverished, but street smart and resourceful she was. She was indeed. Like our forefathers in Egypt requesting that Pharaoh "Let my people go," my mother, armed with a pair of shoes, persuaded a Russian guard to let her husband go in exchange for the used footwear.

When my father crawled out from the dungeon of the jail, we were there to embrace him. He was unrecognizable. He could not walk. He could not talk. He was a broken shadow of a human being. His spirit was shattered. My mother succeeded in propping him up and supporting his frail body. We started walking away from the camp. A short distance later, Papa collapsed. He lay on the ground, sobbing like I have never seen an adult sob, especially not my father! "You go without me. I cannot make it. Leave me here. Go, go. I can't," he pleaded.

My poor mother, thin and fragile, who rarely opened her mouth, who normally shrank into the background, demanded, "Come on, Mendel, we have to go. Let's go!" She gripped me with one hand, my sister with the other, and commanded Papa to lean on her from the back. Her strength at that moment was incredible, and miraculous in her weakened condition. Somehow we all dragged ourselves along the road toward home.

On the way back, there was no transportation in sight. The trains that brought us there were not running. We would walk all day and then stop at night. I have no idea what we ate, but I know that we knocked on the doors of farmers and asked for food along the way. At night we would sneak into the barns and sheds of the peasants and bed down with the chickens and various creepy-crawly creatures.

Everyone was smelly and dirty. I wanted to cry. I was hungry, my feet hurt, and my shoes were full of holes, but I did not cry. I had to be strong for Mama. For two weeks, somehow we stumbled along, knowing that each step took us farther and farther away from the horror of the death camp.

MY FAMILY AFTER LIBERATION, ABOUT 1945. MYSELF ON THE
LEFT AND DITA ON THE RIGHT

At long last, we arrived at our family compound in Tshernovitz. We had made it back home. It was surreal. We had survived—all four of us. We were alive!

PICKING UP THE PIECES

Back home in Tshernovitz, our life was far from stable. Our home and factory compound was occupied by strangers and no longer belonged to us. The new residents of our former home allowed us to stay in a small area of the house in exchange for my mother's services as the cleaning maid.

To add insult to terrible injury, my father had to hide once more, this time from the Russians. The war was not over yet on the Russian Front, and they needed soldiers. They needed moving bodies, no matter how impaired they were. My father kept out of sight as long as possible. As fate had it, the Russian military caught up with him.

One day while rounding up the men in the neighborhood, they grabbed Papa as well. With consternation, we witnessed my father being pushed into the middle of the procession. Again we had to save Papa. Mama once more came to his rescue. We went ahead of the slowly marching soldiers. She directed us to follow her and be silent. She picked a sheltered spot along the winding road to wait for the soldiers marching by. When Papa walked past us, she moved very quickly and in a muffled tone she commanded, "Mendel, don't look behind, stay still, don't move, talk to me."

The *nachalnik* (Russian commander) did not notice that Papa stepped out of the line. Mama kept on talking and holding firmly to my father's arm. I have no doubt that without her strong grip and determination, my father would have stepped back into line. He was a broken, weak shadow of a human being, afraid to disobey.

Once the marching men passed by, my mother signaled to us bewildered girls and we made it back to our makeshift temporary shelter. Mama acted quickly, stared down danger, and saved Papa's life. I'm sure of it. Those who went to the Russian Front never returned.

We sighed with relief, but not for long. I do not know how, but the Russians found out that Papa had deserted and were looking for him. My father, a hunted man, was desperately trying to outwit the Russians. A series of moves would take us to many locations before we could escape to the refuge of Israel.

While on the run, in order to feed us, Papa did different menial jobs on the outskirts of Tshernovitz. I was terribly skinny and malnourished, and everyone was worried that I would become ill. My parents thought I should be fattened up. Papa took me with him to a peasant home in one of the villages where he worked.

The peasant woman of the house was huge and gruff and smelled of sour milk. Her hair hung in greasy ringlets, and her flabby bosom moved in waves under her coarse, stained, sacklike dress. She was in charge of fattening me up. On a daily basis, she would milk her goat and force milk down my throat by holding my head and squeezing my nose tight like my mother used to. I struggled to avoid the warm, foul-tasting solution. My frail body was forced to surrender and take it in—milk and goat hair alike.

Warm, hairy goat milk—gross! But it was food nevertheless, and the mission was accomplished. I was fattened up, and I thrived. Eventually, we moved to Sibiu, in Transylvania, where we lived for two years.

In Sibiu, for the first time, I was able to go to school. I was twelve years old. I had been seven when we fled our home and boarded the train for the camp. My "grammar school" education turned out to be a grotesque experiential life lesson in human cruelty and evil, where I learned about the outer limits of human suffering and stamina.

Somehow, I passed a test and qualified for the fifth grade in a Catholic school in a Catholic country. The language of the country was now Rumanian rather than the German we spoke at home before the war. I was thrilled to be in school. Between "Hail Marys," I looked around to see if there was anyone else who was not wearing a cross. Alas, I was the only one—once again, a marked person.

Our teacher was a heavyset, matronly woman who looked just like an "old maid" schoolteacher was supposed to, with her severe gray bun and wire glasses perched on her beaklike nose. She worked hard as she tried to teach us math and science, and she took me under her wing when she discovered I was good with numbers and scientific concepts.

One day she asked a physics question about Newton's theory of gravity. There was silence; nobody knew the answer. I hesitated. Should I raise my hand and call attention to myself? Lifting my chin defiantly, my heart pounding, vulnerable yet excited, I raised my hand and was called to the blackboard. Hesitating only seconds, I grabbed the piece of chalk and wrote out the correct formula.

The teacher became noticeably animated, waving her pointer at me while addressing the class: "Look at this little Jewish girl. She can't even speak our language and she knows the answer! What's wrong with the rest of you?" This was a peak experience, an imprinted memory, and one of my few recollections of that school. I was different. I was the only non-Christian in the class, yet I was special. I was smart! I was not pretty, but I definitely was smart.

My sister, Dita, was much more adversely affected than I by her experience in the camp. Her adolescence was traumatized. Her schooling was interrupted. At age sixteen, while we lived in Transylvania, she attended an agricultural school called a *hachshara*, a preparatory school for young adults who were planning to immigrate to Palestine. My mother encouraged her to go. "We need to save at least one of us," she vowed quietly. Rumania would not allow Jews to leave the country at that time except for a select few young people who belonged to Zionist organizations. Dita was one of the *Exodus* Jews as depicted in the movie with the same name. Her boat to Palestine was intercepted by the British, sent to Cyprus, and then secreted into Palestine in 1948.

We lived in Sibiu for two years, until I was fourteen. Life was good. I made friends—Cota and Suri, two Jewish girls who lived on our street. They were pretty and they were rich. Suri even had an angora sweater, the height of luxury. The house she lived in looked like a palace to me. Her family was Orthodox. Suri's mother even had a *shaytel* (a wig to cover up her shaved head). According to the Orthodox tradition, when you marry, you shave your head or cover your hair.

One day when I was visiting, her mother had just baked some challah (traditional, braided egg bread). I must have looked hungry, because she said, "Come here, Erica. Would you like to have a piece of bread?" I had never tasted anything so good. The smell of that house with the aroma of fresh warm bread is an indelible memory.

During that period, I still had very few material things. I had but two dresses. For months I alternated wearing them. I had no books, nothing. Once, when I stayed overnight at Suri's house, her mother had my shoes repaired while I was asleep. The next morning, I hurried home and said, "Look, Mama, look at my shoes!" I experienced the smallest gesture of kindness as a huge gift. The most ordinary things—shoes, a slice of fresh bread—were like jewels from heaven. We were alive; we were not freezing; we were not hungry.

I was an adolescent but very slow to develop physically. Suri and Cota had breasts. I was flat, flat like a board. I asked my mother, "Am I ever going to have breasts?" She said, "Someday." She never explained things to me. She didn't express herself. Perhaps, due to malnourishment and who knows what else, my onset of puberty was delayed. I was sixteen before I had my first menstrual period. It was a relatively minor event for me since all of my friends had already experienced this passage to womanhood.

It was no secret that when my mother was pregnant with me, my father wanted a boy for his second child. When I came along, he was so disappointed that for days he did not want to look at me. So I subconsciously became the son my father never had.

Early on, I played with boys—I swam and climbed trees with them. I was determined not to be a sissy like all the other girls. I reacted sharply if anyone said, "You're a girl and you can't do that." I was ambitious. I was driven. I wanted all the options available to boys. I wanted to achieve, and I did. For the sake of clarity, I want to attest that I never experienced gender identity struggles. I definitely felt like a girl, yet I always walked to the beat of my own drummer, with or without society's blessings.

Among my friends and at school, I was a leader. Organizing events and being in charge came naturally to me. It still does. Eventually, I joined a drama group. I acted, sang, and danced. The audience cheered and threw flowers on the stage. I made people look at me. Even though I was Jewish, even though I was short, even though I was "the ugly one," people watched me and applauded. I translated "being different" into "being unique," and I built on that.

As I walked around the town, people would stop me and say, "Are you the little girl who performed last night?" I was a ham—a "kosher ham." I became quite popular. They predicted that I would grow up to be a performer on stage. Their prediction came true. I am producing, directing, and acting on the stage of my life with great vigor.

My sister left the nest when she was sixteen, moving to Palestine as promised after attending the hachshara. I became Mama's sole preoccupation. My mother was very devoted to me, but I never heard a good word or compliment from her.

We were hoping to join Dita as soon as possible. Meanwhile, we relocated to Bucharest, the capital of Rumania, to follow my father in pursuit of a better job. Although Israel was not yet a state, going to Palestine meant that your life would be safe from persecution. Dita made it to Palestine safely and found a husband. She sent us pictures. Her husband, Israel Ghesser, was so handsome. He was a Sabra, an Israeli native. Her letters kept asking, "When are you coming? When are you coming?" But the Rumanian government would not permit us to leave.

PART II

ISRAEL, 1949–1958

ISRAEL: OUR HOMELAND

In 1949, Rumanian emigration policy changed. We were allowed to leave and immigrate to Israel. We could not believe our good fortune. Our long anticipated moment had arrived. We were free to go. It did not matter that we had to leave everything behind but the clothes on our back. Here we were refugees again. But what a difference a destination makes!

We were going to our ancestral homeland, Israel—heaven for the haunted and unwanted Jews in the world!

"We shall never be refugees again," muttered my father.

"Yes," I echoed, "we will finally be with Dita."

I have no recollection of how we made it to the boat. What I do remember is the sea of silent people we encountered on the deck. I could not understand the reason behind the unnerving silence and worried faces. "This should be a happy time," I thought. "We are going to Israel."

I did not understand then as I do now the deep-rooted fear that people who are oppressed and abused experience, hoping for relief from pain but knowing they may encounter more of it.

What if the government of Rumania were to renege on its promise? Lucky for us, Rumania did let us go.

Once the boat departed the shores, words cannot adequately describe the visible joy and exultation of the passengers. Old and young were like untwisted puppets shouting and chanting praise to the heaven above for steering them to the Promised Land. There was silence no more. Laughter and smiling faces were everywhere. When the boat docked on the shores of Haifa, people disembarked, kneeled down, and kissed the ground, the holy ground! What a sight!

When we arrived, my sister had just had a miscarriage. She was bedridden, and her husband, Israel Ghesser, met us at the boat alone. We had not met Israel but recognized him from the pictures Dita had sent. I had learned a few words of Hebrew with a highbrow British accent. Leaning over the railing of the boat, I recognized my brother-in-law. I was enthralled. He was so handsome! I was completely smitten. Never mind my sister. I was excited to see him. In my halting Hebrew, I shouted, "Israel, Israel, I-yay Dita?" which meant, "Where is Dita?" My style of Hebrew was very highfalutin, like Shakespearean English. My brother-in-law thought it was hilarious. He made fun of my Hebrew and laughed loudly at my efforts. Embarrassed and humiliated, I was determined to prove myself to him, to learn Hebrew fast—and I did. I made learning the language of the land my highest priority. I never again wanted to be laughed at for saying, "I-yay Dita."

MY SISTER AND HER HUSBAND, ISRAEL GHESSER, 1949

GETTING EDUCATED

My parents sent me away to an agricultural school for new immigrant girls called Ayanot, in Nes Ziona, a small town southeast of Tel Aviv. In addition to a small payment that my parents had to make, I earned my tuition by working in the school and on the grounds. It was the most wonderful experience of my life, up to that point. I milked cows, picked oranges, and cleaned out horse stalls. At night, we sat around the bonfire and sang poignant Israeli songs. Words cannot adequately describe the gratitude I felt to be there. We worked very hard on the soil by the sweat of our brows. The work was difficult in the hot Israeli sun, but simple rewards such as eating a juicy orange right off the tree made the experience unforgettable.

I was an enthusiastic pioneer. I threw myself into my new existence. I thought the experience was absolutely terrific, including the smell of horse manure! I listened carefully when Hebrew was spoken, read books, and spoke Hebrew whenever possible. The Israeli teachers lived with us and were all around us when we needed them. I went from page to page in the dictionary, writing a list of new words in the right margin, memorizing them day in and day out. Eight months later, I spoke Hebrew fluently.

At night, after a full day of working and studying, I allowed myself the luxury of joining the others around the bonfire. The rest of the time when I wasn't assigned a chore, I studied. Friends urged me to come out and socialize. There were a bunch of young girls having a good time, but I rarely joined them. When I returned to Tel Aviv eight months later, I needed to be able to speak Hebrew with my brother-in-law. I needed to prove myself.

In order for Israel's kibbutzim (collective farms or communes) to thrive and prosper, they needed both men and women. But they could not attract enough women willing to live away from their families and become farmers. The plan was for new immigrant girls, like me, and the other girls in the agricultural schools to be farmed out to the kibbutzim. More than anything else, I wanted to join a kibbutz. That life—working in the soil, basking in the bonfires, and participating in the dancing and the singing—was the life for me. I believed that the kibbutzim were critical to rebuilding the country, and I was determined to do my part. Very determined.

I can be very passionate about causes I believe in. I was such a Zionist: I believed that all Jews should live in Israel, and I saw the kibbutz as the way to build the country. Farm work, where everyone participated and shared equally, was the way to ensure the development of a productive, successful country. But I was still a minor. My parents did not want me to move away from them permanently. They forbade me to join the kibbutz. They stopped payment for my tuition, and I had to return to Tel Aviv. I was miserable and I was angry, very angry.

I learned a tough lesson. Sometimes, no matter what, you just can't make things happen if you depend on others. I remember thinking that in the future, I needed to be in control of my life. I needed not to be dependent on anyone else, ever! To live my life my way was essential to who I am. That kind of resolve was so unheard of for a young woman in those days. I wonder where I got it. Later in life, if Jerry (my husband) had tried to stop me from realizing my professional goals, we would have split up. Our relationship would have been history. But at that time, my parents had the power. There was nothing I could do.

I was devastated to have to leave the idyllic life of the agricultural school and return to Tel Aviv. But a girl does what a girl has to do. On the bright side, when I returned home, I found out that my friends from Sibiu, Suri and Cota, had immigrated to Israel and settled in Tel Aviv. So we met up once again and created a nice little network of young people, and that was a good thing. I lived with my parents in a three-bedroom condominium they owned in Ramat Chen, on the outskirts of Tel Aviv, and I started night school. None of my friends opted to go to high school. Most young people of that era, boys and girls alike, did not seek a high school diploma. Work was valued; education was not. I wanted both.

Money was scarce. I was ambitious and highly motivated, so I had two jobs while attending high school at night. For one job, from 8:00 a.m. to 3:00 p.m., I was working on an assembly line in a cardboard box factory making cartons. We were evaluated on the speed at which we worked. And, boy, did I show them what I could do! I wasn't very popular with my co-workers because I raised the bar.

We were supposed to turn out twenty boxes an hour, but I doubled that. I still remember the resentful looks I received from my co-workers. It did not stop me. I did what was right for me!

Between 4:00 and 6:00 p.m., I was a receptionist in a music school, and from 7:00 to 10:00 p.m. I attended night school. After class, I often studied until 2:00 a.m. I worked very hard. Studying in a language other than my mother tongue was a challenge. All in all, I was a busy girl! I still am.

For three years work and school took up my life. I did not date. I had very little time for a social life. I earned my high school diploma, becoming the only one of my friends who finished high school. Boys were not important to me. Achievement, focus, proving that I was smart—that's what motivated me then and still motivates me now.

My memories of high school are vague. I do not remember my classmates, except one boy who sat behind me in class. He was from Iraq. He would tickle me just to hear me giggle. I giggled a lot. I don't remember his features other than his dark-framed glasses and curly hair. If I am not mistaken, most of my classmates were boys. I did not get close to any of my fellow students. I was there for three years, and I don't remember any faces. The mind is an amazing thing.

YOUNG, SINGLE, AND FREE

High school graduation was an event without fuss. There was no one to applaud me but me. My friends could not relate to my ambitions, and my parents were worried that I would become too smart and never find a husband.

In those early days of the Jewish state, as I previously mentioned, the focus was not on education, especially for girls. Few boys went to high school. Working and building the homestead was the calling of the times.

My Orthodox girlfriends had strict parents and were not permitted to date. My mother allowed our home to be an open house where the girls and boys came to socialize. As long as she knew where I was, and with whom, she trusted me. I did not disappoint her. I was a "good girl" and proud of it.

My friends and I socialized in groups with boys from Rumania. I was popular but completely unimpressed with the boys in our group. I am not sure what I was looking for, but I knew that I had not yet met my life partner. I used to say, "I don't need a man. I will only marry if we can be partners and equals. I don't need to be supported."

Those were early days, before the current wave of feminist thinking. I have no idea where I got this attitude. None of my girlfriends thought like I did, and clearly, I did not get it from my mother. "We women," she would say, "are smart, very smart, sometimes even smarter than men, but we need them. Without them we are nothing." I thought she was wrong. I hoped she was wrong. I definitely proved later in life that she was wrong.

I was seventeen and a half. I had my high school diploma and was ready to join the armed forces. In Israel, then and now, serving in the armed forces is mandatory commencing at age eighteen—two years for girls and three years for boys. For girls to be excused from the military, they either had to be married or claim under oath that they were Orthodox. As for boys, they could be excused on religious grounds only. Many of my girlfriends were getting married. Some claimed they were Orthodox when they weren't. I strongly disagreed with my friends who lied. I was very disappointed in them. This was our country. The army needed us. I wanted to serve my country! I had to. It was my duty!

I know that my mother was proud of me for getting my high school diploma, as she valued education, but there was always a double message: "Study, my child. Education is important. Yet, you might become too smart, and then will you ever find a husband?" But to me, marriage was not important, not yet. No one around me shared my self-reliance. I was very much alone. I was always building the case for being proud of myself. I had no doubt about where I should be and wanted to be. The opportunity to serve my country was a great honor. I wanted to join the army. I was old enough to make my own decisions, and I did. My resolve to decide what was best for me has been my steadfast companion, then and always.

THE ISRAELI AIR FORCE

When I entered military service, my secret goal was to be in the Israeli Air Force, the most prestigious division of the armed forces. The Israeli Air Force was the best of the best. I felt I had the energy and the enthusiasm necessary to be among this elite group. The Air Force had blue uniforms—very impressive. Eventually I told everyone that I was going to join the Air Force. They said, "How are you going to do that? It's very hard to get in. Everybody wants to end up in the Air Force."

I answered, "I'm going to be in the Air Force," and I appeared before the admissions board to make my request.

I have the feeling, and it has often been reinforced, that if I want something badly enough, I can make it happen. Obviously I can be delusional like anyone else—yet it frequently works.

My request was granted. They assigned me to the Air Force. I was in heaven. Here I was, this short little girl who had glanced furtively around a Rumanian Catholic classroom to find that she was the only child without a cross; who had wandered from town to town as a poor refugee; who now, finally at home among Jews, was realizing her dream of serving in the Israeli Air Force.

I stood up straight and proud, thrilled to give myself over to defending my country. Jews surrounded me, and I felt safe. When I was in agricultural school as a new immigrant, my peers complained about the hard farm work. Not me. I did not complain. I rejoiced. This was the kind of exuberance I brought to my military service as well.

In those days, girls were not sent to the front line, and perhaps it is still true today. However, we were trained to use weapons and went through the rigors of boot camp for three months just like the boys did. I remember standing in line, waiting to be measured for my uniform, and receiving a rifle and bag of supplies. I loved it, standing there, tough and determined, in my green khaki uniform. Years later, my husband, Jerry, said that if he had seen me then, he no doubt would have run the other way!

19 YEARS OLD

ISRAELI AIRFORCE

WITH MY MOTHER

PILOT'S SCHOOL

The boot camp was located in the northern part of the country, near Haifa. Many one-story, long buildings served as dormitories for the men and women.

Maneuvers were not coed, but we all ate together in the mess hall. We were awakened daily at 5:00 a.m. by the yells of the sergeant, "ZMAN LAKUM!" ("Time to get up! Up! Up! Up!") It was dark and cold as we piled into the freezing showers. There was no warm water. It was invigorating. The many exercises they had us do were grueling—walking, running, jumping, and crawling.

In the big mess hall, the new recruits complained about the food, but I thought it was fine. I looked at the whiners and complainers and thought to myself, "What's the matter with them? We're here to do a job. We're serving our country. What a privilege!"

We were taught target shooting. Mind you, it's not an easy task. You hold the gun with the butt against your shoulder and fire. The power of the blast is painful. I was black and blue. I must confess that I never was a very good shooter. My aim was far from accurate.

We had to learn how to clean and take care of our guns. We had to disassemble our weapon into all its parts, hunt for every granule of dust, clean and oil every piece, and do it fast. We had to pass inspection every Friday before going home for the weekend.

We also were taught how to detonate grenades and shoot Czechoslovakian machine guns that inspired the Uzi, the famous

Israeli weapon that came into use a few years later. The grenades were scary. You had to count to three, pull out the pin, and throw them with all your might far into the distance.

Then there were the night maneuvers, which I must admit petrified me. We were near the Lebanese border. We had to take shelter close to the ground, which reminded me of the bugs and creepy-crawlies I encountered during the nights of hiding from the Nazis. It was not for the faint of heart. Eventually, after a few weeks of boot camp, we were called upon to serve as border guards and keep the enemy at arm's length. I was very scared. I could hear noises in the dark but could not see whether friend or foe was coming. I was terrified, to say the least, but I never flinched from duty. "Here I am! Yes, sir!"

To this day, as in the past, I don't allow fear to rule me. I'm counterphobic. I take deep breaths and do what has to be done in spite of my fear. On the other hand, I won't invite danger. I don't hang glide or skydive or go river rafting. They all sound too dangerous to me. I don't need to experience everything. Life is too precious to take unnecessary risks.

During boot camp training, the sergeants kept repeating, "Are you ready?! Can you kill the enemy?" They constantly said, "You women, you won't be sent to the front, but you may have to defend the border. You may have to defend your homes and children."

I learned that I was ready and able to protect and defend myself and those close to me. To this day, I know that I could do whatever is necessary to protect my family. I've said many times that if we lived in a dangerous neighborhood infested with gangs or break-ins, I would have no problem owning a gun. I'm very strong. If it is a matter of survival and I deem it necessary, I would have no problem shooting somebody.

After boot camp I was assigned to an Air Force flight school, or *tayeset*, at Ramat David in northern Israel, close to Haifa. I served there from 1954 to 1956. It was an elite school for pilots. Only the best of the best were chosen. Those pilots were tall, smart, handsome, and very privileged. The Israeli Air Force is legendary for its highly skilled, efficient, and streamlined fighting units. Because I

AARON (FRONT ROW, LOWER LEFT), A SPECIAL FRIEND

had a high school diploma, which very few had, I became a big shot. I was put in charge of inventory for airplanes, special rations for pilots, and all of the equipment they needed to function in top form.

I was surrounded by all of those knockout gorgeous pilots in the prime of their youth. The chief officer of the flight school was Ezer Weizman, the nephew of Chaim Weizmann, the first president of Israel, and the brother-in-law of Moshe Dayan, the famous Israeli military leader. Boy, was Ezer Weizman tall and handsome!

I lived too far from home to visit my family more than once a month. On Friday and Saturday nights, I was part of an ensemble that entertained the soldiers who remained on base. Every Friday afternoon, just before the Sabbath, we got all spiffed up—shoes shined, uniforms perfect—and we lined up for inspection. Gorgeous Ezer Weizman himself would walk up and down the rows inspecting all of the soldiers. He had a phenomenal memory. Lined up were young men and women from Yemen, Iraq, Morocco, England, Bulgaria—from all over the world—and he would ask personal questions like, "How is your mother? Is your sister still in Johannesburg? When do you expect she might emigrate? Is your grandmother back home from the hospital?" When he approached me, he never failed to ask, "Will I hear you sing tonight? You sing very well, *chayelet* (soldier)!" He definitely had the personal touch—and such charm and charisma.

I was one of a small number of women in the Air Force. We were thrilled to be surrounded by these impressive pilots, dressed in their navy-blue uniforms and gold braids, so dignified, so intelligent, so brave on their dangerous maneuvers. Naturally, before long, I developed a megacrush on Aaron, one of the pilots I was assigned to take care of. I would be sitting at my phone station; the phone would ring; I would hold my breath, wondering if it was he. Often enough, he would be calling in to ask whether I could get a certain part from inventory or whether his plane was ready. He had a husky, very sexy voice. By the time I finished the call, I was shaking. I was absolutely smitten. He never knew it, and I never let on. Remember, I was smart but not pretty. Why would I think that I could attract one of those handsome pilots?

There were no rules against fraternizing between men and women in the Air Force. It was a casual atmosphere, and I had some very good times, especially socializing in groups. I found that there was safety in numbers. I was not about to get involved, and casual sex was out of the question. I was committed to protecting my virginity. Air Force women often were assumed to have compromised themselves. I decided that no matter what happened, I would not be deflowered.

For one thing, I was very passionate in my fantasy life, and I was afraid I would become a "lady of the night." I kept myself "pure" because I thought, "Once I 'do it,' then I will go from man to man to man," and I didn't like that picture. The only scenario I could imagine was, like the kids say, first base, second base, third base! I did get on base—and got perhaps to second, maybe even third, but that was it. No one told me to keep my virginity. My mother never spoke to me about sex. No one did. I just wanted to be a virgin when I got married, and marriage was the last thing on my mind.

We were given passes from Friday afternoon until Sunday morning. Many of the pilots lived on the base. They all had Vespa motorcycles—shiny, Italian-made machines. Because I worked in the inventory office and was "one of the guys," I joined them often on rides on their Vespas. You should see the Sea of Galilee in the moonlight! The winding road carried us through Nazareth. When the fully covered Arab women carrying baskets full of goods on their heads would see us female soldiers leaning against our male drivers, they would send us looks of outrage. Only eyes peered through their head coverings, but their expressions were still clear. If looks could kill, I would have been a corpse.

That's not the first time I'd received such looks—and they could come from Jews as well as from Arabs. In high school, we made a day trip to a neighborhood of Jerusalem called Mea Shearim. Dressed in shorts, we were walking along the narrow streets with our teacher. Suddenly, out of nowhere, Orthodox Jewish residents of the neighborhood began throwing stones at us. "Shiksas!!" they shouted, spitting at us and using an epithet for non-Jewish women—or Jewish women who are not observant. Our teacher quickly rounded us up and hustled us out of there. I was reminded of the concentration camp, of being attacked by Nazi soldiers, of having to run for dear life—only this time, we were attacked in Jerusalem by religious zealots. We were not "kosher." We showed our legs, which is immodest for women, according to the rules and regulations of Orthodoxy. That we were being stoned in our own land by other Jews was a tragic example of fanaticism, I thought. It was also a commentary on our teacher's lack of sensitivity and awareness. She should have known better! One must respect the customs of others when in their territory. We could have worn long pants on that day trip, just as one can wear slacks instead of shorts in a Muslim country and head coverings in churches or temples where that is the custom. It's a matter of respect.

But the memories of those fun weekends in the Air Force are heartwarming! I will never forget Aaron, my secret love. He was tall, blond, and handsome. I would ride with him, tummy to back, on his motorcycle. We developed a close bond. He was smart and sensitive, and he liked me a lot. He told me so. We were just buddies, though. That's all I could handle. I went out of my way to be unattractive so Aaron would not see me as a potential love object and make advances toward me. Secretly I had fallen head over heels for him, but he did not know it. My message to him was clear: "Don't come close." I was not ready to act on my rich and passionate fantasy life.

The short and long of it was that I was afraid to become intimate with Aaron and that was that. I think he knew it, accepted it, and enjoyed our special but asexual friendship. He alluded in jest more than once that we were bonded for life, were soul mates, and would get married someday. I wanted to believe him, and I did believe him. But he was wrong. Our future together was never to be.

Like other pilots, Aaron worked for many days at a time and then had many days off. When he would go into Haifa with the guys on a pass, he'd be late in returning. I was worried that he would find a girlfriend there because he didn't get "it" from me. I would never know. What I do know is that we continued to be close friends, and I remember those times with such joy.

And sadness.

It was a flight school. The pilots were young and in training, and there were many airplane crashes. These were incredible young men in their prime, but it happened all too frequently. After such tragedies the school would briefly shut down. The dark cloud of death would descend upon us, and we would mourn and mourn some more. I always said to myself, "Hopefully, Aaron won't be on one of them."

Any pilot who was killed was one of our finest. "Who is going to be next?" we would gasp with grief. Immediately, another group of young people would be sent into the air. The missions continued. They had to. In the same vein, I remember walking along the road near the Lebanese border and hearing a shot. Ahead someone had been injured or killed. In such instances, the victims were attended to in a hurry. The injured were transported to the nearby hospital and the dead were taken to the morgue. Then the traffic on the highway resumed as if nothing had happened. The tragedy of war was to become our way of life.

Sometime during my second year on the Air Force base, Aaron was sent on a maneuver and never came back. He was in a plane that was shot down. I was crushed. For a long time, no one else measured up. I will never forgive him for dying on me.

While in the camps as a young child, I had watched those dead bodies rattling along in the open wagons and scattered on the road. But the death of my friend in the Air Force was personal—very personal.

I decided then and there never to get too attached to anyone. The pain that was the price of loss was not worth it. It had worked for me in the past, as a child, and it would work for me in the future, as an adult, I thought. I would never depend on anyone else completely, only on myself. The decision I made then has persisted over time.

On those infrequent weekends when I used my pass to go home for a visit, I usually had to hitchhike. That was how we traveled in Israel in the early 1950s. Traveling from the flight school down to Tel Aviv took close to three hours. Sometimes I got a ride on a plane, and more often on a helicopter. But usually I hitchhiked by myself. I would stand by the road and along would come a huge truck. I had to climb up the high step into the cab, which took considerable strength. I was strong! I was a little powerhouse. I still am.

One weekend, I had just come off night guard duty, which meant long hours of staying awake. As I trudged down the road, thumbing for a ride, fatigue dropped over me like a heavy blanket. A large truck slammed on its brakes and pulled to a stop. "Chay-elet, la'an aht holechet?" "Hey, soldier, where are you going to?" the trucker asked. He was going only part of the way to Tel Aviv, but I took the ride anyway. I knew I would get another ride to my final destination.

I climbed in next to the driver and attempted conversation. I was fighting to keep my eyes open, but I kept nodding off. "Soldier," he pleaded, "please do not fall asleep. I'll sing to you, I'll talk to you—anything you want. I'm tired, too. If you go to sleep, I might fall asleep, too, and then where would we be? Please, don't sleep!" So we started singing to keep each other awake. We sang and sang until we arrived safely at his destination.

I loved going home to visit. When I walked into my mother's kitchen, it was filled with savory aromas. She went to great lengths preparing for me, cooking my favorite meals. It was nice to come home, but after Aaron died, I found myself going through the motions of talking and laughing, like a zombie. I missed Aaron. I lamented about what was and what could have been if he had lived. I could not shed my sadness. I shared it with no one. It was my personal loss.

My friends in Tel Aviv were happy to see me and made small talk. Yet I was judging them, and they knew it. I suppose my parents were proud of me, yet I knew they did not approve of my decisions. I was a young girl. I wasn't married. My mother watched me with dismay. She was terrified that I might end up an old maid. I was always marching to the beat of a different drummer. If they were proud of me, they never said so. I was just too independent for my parents, especially for my mother.

My parents' three-bedroom townhouse in Ramat Chen was in a young neighborhood where new immigrants settled. I was comfortable there. I even had my own bedroom. My father mastered the Hebrew language, as he had Rumanian and Russian before, and landed a prestigious job as an underwriter for an insurance company. My mother did what she always did, taking care of the house and living through my father and her children.

The word was that Papa had always loved the ladies—even back in Tshernovitz. My poor mother watched him like a hawk, always asking him where he had been and why he was late. She was one unhappy woman! I felt bad for her, yet I resented her overinvolvement with me. My sister was out of the house, and my father, for all practical purposes, was not there for my mother, which left me to fill the gap. I had very conflicted feelings about my mother. She always asked where I was and what I had been doing. I was very devoted to her, and part of me liked to include her in my life, to share my experiences with her. But part of me felt burdened by her constant questions. She wanted to know every thought I had and everything I did. She didn't have a life. I wanted to make her happy but never felt I succeeded. As had been the case with her own mother, nothing seemed to put a smile on her face.

My father was self-centered and self-indulgent. He seemed oblivious to my mother's needs. Having fine clothes and getting dressed up were what seemed to matter most to him. He spent a lot of money on himself and was the picture of elegance. Mama, who managed the money, rarely got anything for herself. She was a mess, but she didn't care. She went out of her way to be a slob, I thought. She was very passive. She didn't exist as a viable person in Papa's world. He had a condescending attitude toward her. She existed to serve him, and she passively accepted that role. Papa was charming, the life of the party. He was smart and self-educated. People liked to be around him. Mama was just there.

After the army, when I moved back to my parents' home, I enjoyed a special relationship with my father. We shared a love of deep conversations about important topics such as philosophy, the ways of the world, religion, and cruelty of man toward man. All the while, I felt bad for my mother, who was outside our loop. She was only an observer of these animated discussions. No one stopped her from participating, but she had nothing to say.

My mother rarely shared anything with my father. They had little in common except for the life history of survival, which I assume was a strong bond. I felt the need to be there for her.

I felt I had to "feed" her, at least with attention. She seemed so lonely, and I felt so sorry for her. However, I did not give her the attention she truly wanted. It would not have killed me, but I was young, busy, and ignorant. I regret this so very much. Youth is wasted on the young.

After the army, I dated casually, but the guys in my social circle did not meet my expectations. My mother kept asking, "What's wrong with this one? What's wrong with that one? What's the problem?"

I would say, "Mama! If you like him so much, you marry him. He's not for me."

"God will punish you, the way you talk to me," she'd say.

I'd reply, "What God?" That scared her. She'd exclaim, "Don't say that!"

ISRAELI GOVERNMENT TOURIST INFORMATION OFFICE

After serving in the Air Force, I tried reconnecting with my friends, but I felt like a fish out of water. I didn't belong. They were two years into adulthood. They had moved ahead in their lives. They worked. They had nice clothes. They were married. I had been in the military and had nothing to show for it except rich memories that no one cared about.

Among my friends in Tel Aviv, I was the only one who was not part of a couple. Everyone (my girlfriends, my family) was worried about me. I went out with one guy for a while, but I don't even remember his name. Everyone expected me to marry him, and I probably would have eventually. But I was giving myself one more chance to be unique, to be independent, to experience the world according to Erica. I began looking for a job, and not just any job. I wanted a prestigious position, and I got one. I was hired as a guide in the Israeli Government Tourist Information Office, where I stayed from 1956 to 1958.

When I first set my sights on that job, I knew I had to improve my English. I had studied English in high school, but I wasn't very fluent. I spent hours upon hours studying the language. I mean hours and hours. I spent days with dictionaries, reading books, writing pages and pages of "this means this; that means that," and practicing the language every chance I had, just like I did when mastering the Hebrew language.

Hebrew had been very difficult for me to learn because the language does not use Latin letters. It didn't relate to any of the European languages I knew. In English, the letters are the same as German or Rumanian letters, so learning English was not as hard as learning Hebrew. I studied English with the same intensity I brought to everything else. After all, I had learned Russian, Rumanian, and Hebrew. *Try to stop me!* I thought.

What a job! I was given a desk in a lovely office in Tel Aviv, on Ben Yehuda Street next to the well-known Hotel Dan. I greeted tourists from all over the world and answered their questions. The tourist office was not a travel agency, but we assisted tourists with their itineraries when we had time and interest. I was very good at my job. I could understand the Americans, but the British, with their Cockney accents—that was another story. I loved my job and the prestige of sitting at my desk across from tourists, smoking American cigarettes, troubleshooting if they had complaints, and helping them with their sightseeing schedules.

Occasionally I heard complaints about Israel from American Jewish tourists, who often had unrealistic expectations of Israelis. I hate to say this about some Jews because stereotypes can be damaging. American Jews are generous. They make large donations to good causes and so forth. Many of them came to Israel representing B'nai B'rith, Hadassah, and other Jewish agencies. Because they gave big donations and now were traveling in Israel, they had an attitude of entitlement. They would report, for example, that cab drivers were "taking them for a ride."

"Israel is a Jewish state," they would lament. "This is our country, yet the cab drivers are dishonest and take advantage. These are our brothers and sisters. How can this happen in Israel?"—as if the Holy Land was made up of holy people.

I was only twenty-two, but I thought such expectations were so naive. The concept of a "Holy Land" and "holy people" is a myth. As in other countries of the world, cab drivers will charge whatever they can when tourists don't know what's what. Many American Jews expected more respect and solidarity from their Israeli kinsmen. I listened to their complaints and was amazed at their grievances. I thought, "You're a tourist, and tourists are marks. They can be taken advantage of." In Israel, the prevalent myth was that all Americans are rich. In America, money grows on trees, we thought. People will be people, no matter where they are.

I'm reminded of a famous Jewish writer and philosopher of the early twentieth century, Achad Ha'am, who said, "When will we know we have a country? When we have thieves, police officers, everything the rest of the world has—then we will know we have a country." He was right. No country in the world is an island. Israel and its people are special and unique, yet similar to other countries in the Western Hemisphere.

I heard another complaint that is worth mentioning, from a man who was traveling with his mother. Next door to our office at the Hotel Dan, ladies of the night were roaming the streets. The man was so irate when he discovered that prostitutes were part of the scenery: "In Israel—in the Holy Land—there are prostitutes?" I think he was a mama's boy, poor baby. I felt like the mother hen, sitting there soothing ruffled feathers.

Part of my job, in addition to imparting information, was to accompany private tourist agencies all over Israel, rating their performance and the sites they chose. The Israeli Government Tourist Information Office made sure that the agencies they recommended maintained the highest standard in the industry.

Back in the office, dressed smartly in a tailored business suit,

I greeted distinguished visitors from all over the world. Fortified with the firsthand experience I gathered while accompanying the private travel agencies, I was able to guide our visitors with confidence. I felt worldly and sophisticated in my multifaceted job. I really enjoyed meeting people from around the world. The tourists responded to me in kind. I was their first contact in the Holy Land, and they told me they enjoyed being in my presence. I was enthusiastic, informative, and genuinely glad to host them.

It was against government regulations to accept gifts from tourists, except for cigarettes. Most of them smoked, and, of course, they offered me some. Smoking added just the right touch of sophistication. In those days, cigarettes in Israel were manufactured from strong, smelly Turkish tobacco. By contrast, American Kents were truly light and flavorful. I smoked them every chance I got. I was hooked. I blame American tourists for my nicotine addiction. It's their fault!

Since I lived at home with my parents, I was able to save money. I dated casually so that when there were parties, I had an escort. We never went to restaurants because they were too expensive. Nobody had cars. Local buses took us everywhere.

For fun, we had parties in one another's homes, and we danced and danced some more. My dancing partner was Harry (or was it Barry?). I loved dancing. I vowed to myself that I would never marry anyone who was not a dancer. (Alas: Jerry, my husband, is many things, but a dancer he is not. He has two left feet, but he is a good sport. On cruises and at weddings and parties, he accommodates me by just standing there and hanging on while I do the leading. He follows along with a shuffle here and a shuffle there. It's truly hilarious.)

While my work at the tourist office was exciting, my love life was so-so. After Harry, I dated Moshe. I liked him and he loved me. My parents thought he was terrific! I dated him for a long time, but we were never intimate. Going to bed was not an option for me. The heart-pounding passion I felt for Aaron, although thrilling, was not comfortable. At that stage of my life, I just didn't let it happen. Moshe wanted to marry me. He waited and waited and then finally married a friend of mine.

I was the envy of many of my friends. I was single. I was in charge of my own life. I had to answer to no one, and life was good. Since I lived at home and did not have to pay rent, I allowed myself some luxuries. I had a tailor—my own tailor! There were no department stores. Imagine that! At my tailor's shop, I chose the fabrics and designed my own clothes. Now I had a place to wear clothes that supported my new self-image, "dressed for success," as they say now.

Not having a car was not a big deal for me. Let me put it this way: I did not know any better. I would leave for work early in the morning and walk the entire distance into the city. It was a stretch—about an hour's walk each way. My stride was purposeful and confident. I felt the pride of accomplishment. Never mind my friends with their husbands. There was nothing special about them. I walked to work those many blocks in my new clothes with such self-satisfaction.

The tourist office had an arrangement with the British government involving their military base on Cyprus. When soldiers stationed there had vacation time coming, they would spend it in Israel. Several of us single girls were called upon to entertain them, to be their escorts for the evening—completely chaste, of course! Next door to our office, a nightclub flourished, mainly for tourists. Israelis didn't have money to spend on nightclubs. In our office, the word would go out, "OK girls, who's available on Saturday night? A few soldiers have reservations at the nightclub next door." Here was another chance to speak English. The atmosphere in the nightclub was exotic and attractive. It was dark, with music and dancing. The food was different and interesting, and free, to boot.

One night I was there with the British soldiers and a group of colleagues including Dorit, an immigrant from France. She was single, and we had become friends. She was a party girl, cute and blond, with a little turned-up nose. At the nightclub, we were having a good time dancing and singing. Dorit ordered an appetizer.

I took a bite and asked, "What is it?"

She laughed and replied, "They're oysters."

I started to gag. I didn't know what to do. I already had it in my mouth, so either I would swallow it or throw up. Somehow it stayed down. To this day, I would never knowingly eat these creepy-crawlies of the sea.

Dorit occasionally found dates for us. My married friends were worried about me, and very protective. Obviously, they didn't understand the kind of life I was leading. Now, as I look back, I think Dorit probably moved in the fast lane. We were friends for a while, until I figured out that the fast lane was not for me and that hanging out with my married friends and occasionally dating single, nice guys was the safer road to choose.

One blind date stands out in my mind. On this particular occasion, Dorit found two guys from Jerusalem on a truck. I have no idea where she found them. She was sitting in the front with one of the guys; the other one was supposed to be for me. My date and I were sitting in the back of the open truck.

Well, my date that night was a Sabra (native Israeli)—what a knockout! His name was also Moshe. I could have gone for him, but he was from Jerusalem, too far away. He was tall and rugged. Many Sabras were very handsome and swashbuckling but had no manners. Israelis in general have a reputation, especially among Americans, for being that way. War children, you see, don't have time for niceties.

So there we were, sitting together in the back of a pickup truck going somewhere. We were singing a song or something. Suddenly, he took off his shoe. I was surprised to see a torn sock with his toe sticking out. He took off his sock, scratched his foot, put his sock and shoe back on and continued singing.

I said, "Moshe, aren't you embarrassed to take off your shoe with a torn sock and scratch yourself?"

He looked at me as if I came from outer space. "But it's itching," he said, implying, "Wouldn't everybody do the same?"

He was a typical Sabra. Although I was raised European, in a culture where manners mattered, I found that outlook so refreshing, even though it was foreign to me.

When I first arrived in Israel and was surrounded by Israelis, I tried to emulate them. They stood tall; never mind being polite and proper. They were *dugri* (direct)—what you saw was what you got; what they thought, they said. You always knew where you stood with them. They didn't observe social etiquette. They didn't intentionally hurt someone's feelings, but if they did so accidentally, so be it. At home in their own land, they did not kowtow to anybody. They didn't have to hide because they were Jewish. They did not have to watch every word and gesture. I loved this attitude. I emulated their style.

Being outspoken and straightforward suited my temperament. I liked that part of me. Although my roots are European (where you mind your manners and are careful of others' feelings), the Israelis had a more natural, authentic way of being—yes, even crude at times. It made sense to me. There was no phoniness, no games, no surprises. It felt safe knowing what to expect.

MARRIAGE? NOT YET

I don't even remember the names of most of the potential husbands everyone tried to pair me up with. At one point I said to myself, "I'll probably marry Harry; he is a really nice guy. But before I settle down, I want to go to America and visit my sister." I was not in a hurry to get married. Harry was not to be. My life would not be in Israel.

My sister, Dita, her husband, and their two children had moved to Los Angeles while I was in the Air Force. They had struggled to make a living in Israel. Dita's mother-in-law, Rivca, had come to Los Angeles to visit an elderly aunt named Bayla. When she decided to stay in America permanently, she urged her son, Israel, to immigrate to the States as well, which he did. Aunt Bayla was a woman of means, and she promised my sister and her family their own home and an opportunity to make a nice living. True to her word, after six months, Bayla helped them buy a duplex in the Fairfax area of Los Angeles. Israel found a good job and the family settled in.

AN UNCANNY PREDICTION

I was twenty-four, still single, had money saved, and decided to visit Europe, as well as my sister in Los Angeles. I wanted to travel before getting married and settling down. A young woman traveling alone was unheard of at that time.

IN ISRAEL, 1957, MY FRIEND LUCHI (LEFT)
AND MYSELF, TWO CAREER GALS

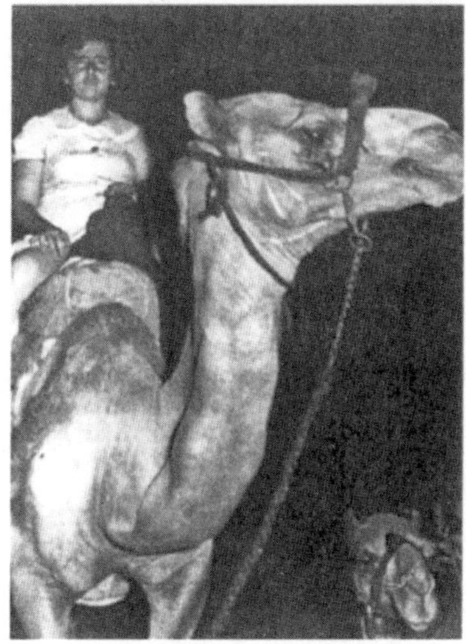

AT A BEDOUIN CAMP, 1957
(SEE INVITATION IN APPENDIX)

A traveling psychic from Haifa was scheduled to be in Tel Aviv about two months before my visit to America. I have always been intrigued by the paranormal, by psychic phenomena. I have already mentioned my mother's psychic abilities. Also, my sister visited a psychic when she came to Israel. Some predictions actually happened, including the death of a close friend of hers, a young man named Yidale. When the traveling psychic came to Tel Aviv, six friends and I prebooked appointments. Readings had to be scheduled far in advance.

Each of us went separately, and then we got together and shared what we were told. That particular psychic was the one who predicted the Sinai War and that a cure for cancer would be discovered in Israel.

I was always skeptical and suspicious of what I could not understand, but nevertheless I was intrigued. At my reading the psychic said, "You really want to live in this country. This is where your heart is, but this is not where you are going to end up. You are going to live somewhere far away, over a long, long ocean. Before the end of this year, you will be on a boat sailing toward your destiny. You are going to marry a widower and you are going to have two children. Your future is not in Israel. It is over the ocean."

I came out of that session and cried like a baby. It was so far off the mark, I felt, and yet why was I sobbing? Somehow, deep within me, I believed her. I knew she was right. But it was crazy. Why would I marry a widower? It made absolutely no sense.

It was October of 1958, so only two months of the year remained. In those days it was very difficult to get a visa, especially for single women, because the country didn't want to lose its women. They tended to leave and never return.

I knew many Israelis who left and never came back. I used to sit in judgment. I did not approve of Israelis who traveled abroad and never returned. "Look at them. They're traitors," I thought. Yet, a part of me that I didn't know or understand, something deep within, was touched. After sharing our readings, my friends and I all questioned the psychic's predictions. We all thought she was way off track. We could not fathom that some of her predictions would truly happen, but they did. They did indeed.

Back at my office, I requested a month's leave of absence as soon as I could get a visa. I told my colleagues that I planned to go to Europe and then to the United States to visit my sister. They agreed and prepared a letter for the American consul stating that I could have my job back upon my return.

At the window of the American consulate, I presented my Israeli passport and the letter from my employer in order to start the procedures to obtain my visa. As I was leaving, I met an acquaintance in the hallway and stopped to chat. Suddenly, the consulate's clerk hurried up to me. "The American consul wants to see you," she said.

Wondering what was wrong, I walked into his office. He was a tall, handsome young man with a crew cut and a wonderful

American accent. He stood up and shook my hand. "Have a seat," he gestured, as he looked at the letter from the Israeli Government Tourist Information Office. He looked at me over the glasses on his nose. "So you want to go to America," he said.

"No, not just to America," I corrected him. "I want to go to Europe, and then I want to visit my sister, who lives in Los Angeles."

He put down the letter from my employer, tipped back his chair, took off his glasses, and chewed on one handle. "You speak English," he said, making it sound like a criticism. "If you leave, what's the guarantee that you will come back? You could teach Hebrew School. You could work for American Jewish agencies. You could get married, and you may never come back."

I looked him straight in the eye. "Why would I not want to come back? Remember, I'm single. I am working for the government in the tourist office. I meet a lot of American men visiting here. I could have my pick. If I just wanted to leave the country and live in America, I could have been married by now." I maintained eye contact. "I believe very strongly," I continued, "that all Jews should live in Israel. I'm positive that my life is here in this country."

He straightened up, placed my letter in a folder. "OK," he said, and signed my papers on the spot. I now had the permission to leave the country any time I wanted.

I returned to my office and announced excitedly, "Hooray! I have my visa papers. I can now contact my sister, and you will need to replace me for a few weeks."

Mr. Antman, the director of our agency, was astonished. "What happened," he wanted to know, "between you and the American consul?" It was unheard of to get a visa on the spot.

My friends were so happy for me. They knew that I had been saving money for a long time. A year earlier my friend Kutsa had been trying to buy a condo and needed a little more money for the down payment. She asked if I would loan her the money. I said, "Of course, you can have the money until I go on my trip." She promptly paid me back when I needed it.

I was just about to embark on my journey when an American journalist, Anita Philips, came to our office.

She wrote articles for the travel section of the *Los Angeles Times*. This was her first visit to Israel. As we talked, I told her about my plans to visit my sister in Los Angeles, but that first I would go to Naples, Venice, Rome, Vienna, London, and New York. She got very excited.

"What a coincidence," she exclaimed. "I'm also going to Venice, Naples, and Rome. I bought a car, a little Renault. Why don't we meet in Italy and travel together?"

That's what we did. She also gave me her mother's address in Los Angeles so that I could look up her mother when I arrived. Anita had to stay behind for her assignment.

I loved my trip to Europe. I spent about nine days visiting Naples, Venice, and Rome with Anita. I then went on my own to Vienna, where I spent some time with my cousin Hadi.

I visited the Israeli Government Tourist Information Offices in all the European cities on my itinerary. I went on local tours. I stopped in London and Glasgow and then flew to New York. New York was very, very cold—it was wintertime. My tear ducts gave way and little water driblets gushed down shamelessly on my frozen cheeks. Whenever my eyes water unexpectedly in cold weather, I recall New York in wintertime with fondness.

From New York, I flew to Los Angeles. What a sight from above! The city looked like a glittering, precious jewel.

I saw Anita, the American journalist and my European travel companion, only a few times over the years. To my regret, we lost touch. She has been out of sight, but not out of mind.

PART III

AMERICA, 1958

THE LURE OF LOS ANGELES

It was December 1958. Flying low over the City of Angels as we approached the airport, I was awed by the panorama—the hugeness of it all, the glamour of it all. I was so impressed!

I moved in with my sister, Dita, and her family. She took me around to meet their friends and introduced me to single people, especially men. Before I left Israel, my friends got together and bought me a present. When I opened it on the boat, I saw the enclosed note: "Marry yourself an American and bring him back to Israel." They knew that my heart wasn't with the guy I had been dating. They also knew that my heart was dedicated to a life in Israel. There are quite a few Americans living in Israel, but for me, it was never to be.

My brother-in-law was instrumental in my decision to stay in America. He encouraged me to date, have fun, and perhaps find a husband. At first I would hear none of it, but eventually, with reluctance, I wrote to my employer and asked for an extended leave of absence for a few more months. I decided then and there to go through the motions and humor my brother-in-law, who hoped that I might find a husband and stay in America.

JEWISH MATCHMAKERS

My brother-in-law put his money where his mouth was. He set me up with a Jewish matchmaker called Kurt of California. A parade of dates began to appear regularly, and I started to enjoy myself. I was still determined to return to Israel, but my brother-in-law pointed out that I had nothing to lose by dating. I could see the city and have a good time. I barely remember most of those dates. A few stand out in my mind.

One is "short Jerry" (not to be confused with my husband, Jerry).

Short Jerry was a nice guy. He liked me a lot. He wanted to take me to meet his mother. That suggested a closeness we didn't have and made me uncomfortable. But he insisted, and I gave in. "What the heck," I thought. It felt nice to be wooed. Before he took me to meet his mother, he asked me if I would mind shaving. In those days, I didn't shave my underarms. That's not what women from Europe or Israel did back then. I must have had a bushel of hair in my armpits! I didn't mind shaving when Jerry asked me to. I met his mother and sister. They liked me. I was a nice kosher girl from Israel. We continued dating for several weeks.

But, short Jerry was not to be. Tall Jerry, my husband, would eventually enter my life.

Before I met my husband, there was a man I had an interest in. I viewed him as a potential contender. He was also a referral from Kurt of California. He was older, mature, and he wanted to get married. He was in the import/export business. He wined and dined me and made me feel special. There was a certain intrigue about him. He attended mysterious meetings at the Sunset Strip Hotel while I waited in the coffee shop. I'm positive he was wheeling and dealing in secret, maybe illegal activities having to do with Mexico. But he knew how to treat a lady. He was patient and respectful. I laid it all out for him from the outset: I said I was saving myself for marriage, so if he wanted sex right away, I wasn't the one. He said he had plenty of ladies to have sex with. He was looking for something permanent, like a wife. Sex can wait, he said. He was very generous, throwing around hundred-dollar bills at Lawry's in Los Angeles, an expensive restaurant where everybody knew him. I was flattered to be in his company.

I was enjoying myself and began thinking of him as a potential mate. But my suspicions grew when he would disappear for days or weeks, and I didn't know where he was. Sure enough, after six months or so, he completely dropped out of sight and never returned. He dropped me just like that, no warning, no explanation. I had been sucked in by his charm and special treatment.

Looking back, I can see that he was a fast operator. He used to meet with two or three men, and when I would ask about the meeting, he would say, "It's just business." Quite a bit later, someone ran into his sister, who said he "couldn't do it" to a nice girl like me. So whatever his scam was, I was spared.

Then there was the one memorable date, recommended by a distant relative, that was over before it started. He was supposed to be a gentleman but turned out to be anything but. We were at a hotel, dining and dancing, when he suggested we go upstairs.

"What do you mean, upstairs?" I asked.

"Well, I've wined and dined you. How many more dates do we have to have before we go to bed?"

"I don't go to bed," I told him. He looked astonished.

"Who are you kidding? You were in the Israeli army. Do you want to tell me you are still a virgin? Do you see hair standing straight up on the palm of my hand? That's how likely it is that you are a virgin."

I stopped in my tracks. "Take me home," I said calmly.

Back at my sister's house, he didn't even get out of the car and open the door for me. Quite a gentleman!

Next in line was Max, a cousin of my brother-in-law. Max lived in Nebraska, and whenever he visited Los Angeles, he took me out. He was generous and thoughtful. He treated me with kid gloves. I don't think I could have continued to evolve into my own person had I married him. He was twenty years my senior and saw me as this naive little Israeli girl. In Nebraska, he had been involved with a Christian girl. His parents were Orthodox Jews, so Max couldn't disappoint his parents and marry her. I was the answer to his parents' prayers. Max was tall, and I liked him. At the time, I could see myself married to him.

Then I met Jerry Miller. A friend of my sister's, a woman named Bena, was visiting from Israel. She was at temple on the High Holidays. Jerry was sitting with his mother in the next pew. Bena saw this good-looking young man, struck up a conversation, and asked if he was single. She said, "Boy, do I know a nice girl from Israel." On the other side of Jerry sat an American woman who let it be known that she had an eligible granddaughter. On that fateful High Holiday morning in 1959, Jerry got two phone numbers: one for a visiting Israeli girl and one for a local American girl. Of course, he called the American girl first. Then he decided to check out the Israeli girl, too.

The parade of eligible men had come and gone until the night Jerry Miller first rang the doorbell. As prearranged, my brother-in-law would go to the door and let my date in. This time he gave me the thumbs-up sign—meaning "this one is special." Jerry was tall and slender and wore a brown suit. He looked good! I knew right away that he was a prime candidate. He was serious and reserved. He was Jewish. He was intelligent. He was a college graduate and he happened to have a car, too. Material things never meant much to me, but a car in Los Angeles was a nice bonus. I knew I could learn to love him. Money was not an issue, but seriousness of purpose and education were. Jerry had been a high school teacher. He had taught business and typing. He had graduated from the University of Southern California (USC) and earned his teaching credential from the University of California–Los Angeles (UCLA).

On our first date, Jerry said, "Let's go to a movie." I said, "I don't want to go to a movie. I want to get to know you." He never forgot that. He was impressed by my assertiveness. He realized that I wasn't at all what he had envisioned—a foreigner, something like a geisha, who would kowtow to him—but that I was a person of substance with a mind of her own, and he liked it. I was plain. I didn't wear makeup. If someone wanted to marry me, I mused, it would be for my brains, not my looks. Jerry apparently cared as little as I did about superficialities. He needed someone who was strong, understanding, and emotionally supportive. And those, indeed, I was. Also, as it happened, I was at a point in my life where I felt that it was time to get married.

But Jerry was hurting. He was still in mourning. His wife, a dietitian, had died rather suddenly of complications from pregnancy, nine months into their marriage. They had purchased a house and were looking forward to their first child. Everything was wonderful. Then suddenly she started hemorrhaging, was rushed to the hospital, and died before Jerry could get there. He was devastated.

This tragedy occurred two or three years before we met, but he was far from over it. Early in our marriage, when Jerry and I joined a gourmet club, another couple knew Jerry's first wife. The woman told me that Jerry's wife had been advised that she shouldn't have any children because of some problem with her fallopian tubes. But when you are young and so much want a family, you think that nothing bad will happen to you. She had never told Jerry she was at risk with the pregnancy. The sudden death of Jerry's wife and unborn child was a tragedy he overcame with great difficulty, if he ever truly overcame it.

While dating Jerry, I was still dating Max from Nebraska. Whenever Max came to town, I put Jerry on hold until Max left. I was willing to marry either of these fellows. I knew I could learn to care for either of them.

The practical side of me would push a romantic notion way into the background. Romance had no part in my choice of a mate. Jerry was younger, and maybe he appealed to the therapist in me. I wanted to help him heal and move on with his life— hopefully with me. So we dated. We had a good time. We also had deep discussions about the ways of the world, politics, business, and opportunities. We never talked about his deceased wife. That door was closed to me. I respected his silence.

I continued to live with Dita and Israel. Dita was working as a hostess at Tam O'Shanter, a restaurant in Los Feliz, a bedroom community near Hollywood. Israel was very controlling. He wouldn't let her learn how to drive and dominated her in other ways as well. I felt that his treatment of her was unacceptable. He was not her boss. He was not her father. How could he not let her do things? So I started butting in. Instead of helping my sister hold her ground and feel empowered, I interfered and told my brother-in-law off. Mind you, I was a guest in his house.

Looking back, I recognize that my sister was very passive. She would say, "What can I do? It is what it is. This is my lot." For the most part, that is no longer the case. My sister has learned over the years to assert herself with family members.

One day Israel said to me, "If you don't like it here, why don't you move out?" I said, "Fine," and I moved out. I did not blame him. I would have done the same if someone were interfering in my life the way I was in his.

I got myself a little apartment around the corner in which I shared a bathroom with an elderly man. Later, Jerry said he rescued me from sharing the toilet with this old man. But it was no big deal to me. I had my own place. I was out of that tense atmosphere in my sister's house. I could not stand witnessing the disrespectful interaction between my sister and her husband!

When I moved out of my sister's house, I still had three hundred dollars of my savings left. I applied for a position at an insurance company. I got the job and worked in an office that provided the income I needed for food and shelter.

A BIG DECISION, AND A BIG QUESTION: AM I A TRAITOR?

As I said before, Dita's husband, Israel, was determined to find me a husband so that I would stay permanently in America. The *schatchen* (matchmaker) and others kept on supplying eligible bachelors to make it happen. I was starting to be convinced that I should stay, but the idea was a double-edged sword. I was in conflict and felt very guilty. I was torn, yet I knew I needed to take charge steered and aided by my cognitions, not my emotions.

Years before, when I lived in Israel, I wanted to become a medical doctor. In fact, it was a childhood fantasy of mine that came about during my time in the camps, when we were all delousing one another. There was this old woman. She was wailing. She was in such terror and pain. I remember thinking, "My gosh, I would like to help her. I would like to help her feel better." As I got older, I still wanted to help people. In order to do so, I wanted to become a doctor. But medical school was only a dream. There was no medical school in Tel Aviv. The only one in Israel at that time was in Jerusalem, and one had to attend full time. We had no funds. When I came to Los Angeles and saw the possibilities, staying was just too tempting. Like the tiger after its first taste of blood, I wanted more. As captain of my life, I navigated the storm of my thoughts and decided to stay in Los Angeles, to anchor my present and future "in the land of the free."

I felt like a traitor. I used to be very judgmental toward Israelis who left for faraway places to make a new life, an easier life, for themselves abroad. I believed that all Jews should immigrate to Israel and build a nation. Now I had decided not to return. I had nightmares. For years, I refused to become a U.S. citizen, even after I married and had children. Family and friends kept asking, "What if there is a war with Israel? You have a family now and have obligations to them!"

Finally, I went through the process and became an American citizen, feeling guilty because I didn't practice what I preached. Today, I no longer believe that all Jews should be in Israel. First, the country is too small to house all of us, and second, the political and financial support of Jews in the Diaspora (outside the Land of Israel) is essential to Israel's survival. As far as my parents were concerned, if staying in America was a prerequisite for my getting married, it was OK with them.

I called the tourist office in Tel Aviv and resigned from my job. With purpose and vigor, I started my new life. I registered at the University of Judaism on Sunset Boulevard in Los Angeles and graduated a few years later with a degree in Hebrew school education. My thinking was that at least I would be teaching Hebrew to American children. In spite of the misgivings about my decision, I felt that the pool of opportunities here was such that I had to seize the moment. If I were not to take care of me, who would? Interestingly, I stumbled upon a book that dealt with my dilemma, *The Art of Selfishness*, by Arthur Seabury.

The book's premise is, "Take care of self first before you can take care of others." A good thing, I thought. "Yes, yes, that's me." We have an attitude in this country that selfish is bad—maybe a Judeo-Christian idea. Actually, selfish means to take care of oneself. In airplanes the instructions are to strap yourself in first and then take care of your youngster. Take care of yourself first so that you can take care of others. If you neglect yourself, there is nothing left to give to others. You can easily become a victim—"poor me"—and that was not who I wanted to be.

GETTING TO KNOW JERRY MILLER

I met Jerry in 1959, and we dated for eight months. For me, the courtship with Jerry centered on the trauma of his loss, the death of his young wife. I made him my project. I wanted to heal him. I wanted to take care of him. I liked Jerry a lot. He was intelligent, creative, and informed; had a sense of humor; and was very ambitious. The practical side of me took over. I believed he was a "good catch" and that we could make a life together.

I enjoyed being with Jerry. I did not have a wild crush, but I had warm, affectionate feelings for him. Although I had several crushes on other men before and after I met Jerry, I decided it was time to get married. I knew I would come to love him and would develop loyalty and commitment. To me, when you get married, you are a couple. You are loyal. You build a nest together. Over time you grow as individuals and as a couple. You grow old together. Is that an outdated, old-fashioned concept of marriage? Perhaps, but it worked for me! I am still married to the same man more than fifty years later, and the relationship is as strong as ever. The pluses outweigh the minuses.

At the time, however, Jerry not ready to commit. He was ambivalent, afraid to make the decision to get married again. I was no longer interested in just dating around and was willing to risk losing him. In addition, I had received a marriage proposal—from Max. One night, I told Jerry, "We have been dating for about eight months. If by now you don't know whether we can have a life together, you won't know it in two years, either. Therefore, you need to decide now, or this is the last time you will be seeing me."

He looked at me in disbelief and said, "Please, give me a week to think it over." (For the record, Jerry remembers asking for a couple of months.) He came back with a "yes." He was afraid to lose me. For all practical purposes, I proposed to him. I asked for his hand—very unladylike. I am glad I did.

Once Jerry and I made up our minds to get married, I decided it was time to have sex. I was now committed to my future husband. Finally, I was ready to give up control.

I never could understand letting go completely. The issue is control, and it is essential to me. The opposite of control is submission, death. One of my close friends in Israel was part of an Orthodox family. She had a 7:00 p.m. curfew, but it didn't keep her from having sex with her boyfriend in the afternoon. She got pregnant and had an abortion, which was unheard of in Israel at that time. She used to say to me, "I cannot help it . . . when he touches me, ahh—" I said, "What does 'ahh' mean?" The way she described being aroused and helpless, unable to resist, stuck in my mind. You have to have your wits about you always. How could a person let herself go so completely?

The nonevent aspect of first-time sex was surprising to me. I had saved myself for my husband, and yet there were no fireworks, no bells ringing, and no recognition of such a momentous occasion. I really do not think Jerry knew I was a virgin. Later when I mentioned it to him, he looked at me, puzzled. He did not expect me to be a virgin, nor did he care, and therefore, in his mind, I wasn't.

From Jerry's Perspective:

Erica and I met on a blind date. At our first meeting,
as I stood in the doorway, she asked, "What would you
like to do this evening?" I suggested we go to a movie.
She said, "No, I don't want to go to a movie. We can't
get to know each other." Then and now, she comes

straight to the point. Erica was the first Israeli I had ever met, and I wasn't used to someone being so direct. I soon learned that she spoke her mind, and I didn't have to guess where she stood. That was OK with me. So I took her to the Mexican Village (neighborhood), where they had dancing—not even knowing how very much she loved to dance. It was a very nice evening and the beginning of six or seven months of dating pretty regularly, but not exclusively. One day she said (with her customary candor), "Jerry, I have good news for you. Someone else has asked me to marry him. I prefer marrying you, but I would like a decision." I said, "Well, give me two months to think about it, and I'll let you know." That was much too long for her to wait. Within a couple of weeks, we decided to get married and we set the date.

GETTING MARRIED: A HILARIOUS BEGINNING

We began making wedding plans. My parents were still in Israel, so my sister; her mother-in-law, Rivca; and Aunt Bayla did everything for me. Bayla was religious and knew an Orthodox rabbi in the Fairfax area, Rabbi Twersky. He spoke Yiddish, Hebrew, and Polish—no English. He agreed to officiate at the ceremony.

We invited a handful of family and friends who resided in Los Angeles.

The date set for my wedding was June 5, 1960. As dictated by Orthodox law, the day before the wedding, I was required to go to the *mikvah* (ritual cleansing bath). Unfortunately it was Friday, the day many Orthodox women went to be cleansed. Mikvahs may be cleaner today, but my experience of dunking in the mikvah water was gross. First they cut my nails to the bone, and then I was immersed in the cloudy, murky water. But the water wasn't murky enough not to see pubic hair floating around. Well, a girl does what she has to do for her man!

On the day of the wedding, my brother-in-law took me to an Israeli hairdresser to have my hair done and asked me to get dressed in my simple yet attractive white wedding dress and wait for him. He was supposed to pick me up at 1:00 p.m. and escort me to the wedding site. The ceremony was to take place at 2:00 p.m. at a little synagogue in the Fairfax district of Los Angeles. To my brother-in-law, as to many Middle Easterners, time means nothing. One o'clock came and no brother-in-law.

I did not know where the synagogue was. I did not know where I was. My sister did not have a telephone. I had no way of contacting anyone. So there I sat, with my fancy hairdo and wedding dress, continuously looking out the window. The hairdresser tried to comfort me, to no avail. I am a very punctual person, and to be late to one's own wedding is very unnerving, to say the least.

I could do nothing but sit and wait. An hour went by and no sign of Israel. Two hours went by. It was almost four o'clock when he showed up. He had gotten lost on Hollywood Boulevard while showing his aunt the sights.

Meanwhile, Jerry was waiting at the altar with the guests. Understandably, he thought I had gotten cold feet and changed my mind. "Well, those things happen," said Dov Katz, an Israeli friend of the family.

Jerry was ready to leave, but Murray Kay, an American friend of his, said, "Jerry, let's wait awhile longer. Maybe they got lost. Maybe they were delayed for some reason." Two hours is a long time to wait at the altar, but Jerry agreed to allow a little more time.

Finally, I arrived. I walked in and saw the aged rabbi with his long beard; Jerry, who was pale and upset; and my sister, who was frantic. We stood under the *chuppah* (wedding canopy).

The ceremony was in Hebrew and Yiddish and was conducted according to Orthodox liturgy. Jerry understood neither. My family is not Orthodox, I'm not Orthodox, Jerry is not Orthodox, but Dita's mother-in-law was Orthodox. The Orthodox rituals dictated the ceremony.

The rabbi told Jerry in Yiddish to walk around me three times in one direction, then three times in the other direction. Jerry didn't understand; he was so *verblunget* (Yiddish for greatly confused). When he was told to go to the left, he went to the right.

When he was told to go to the right, he went to the left. I tried to correct him, and then he would reverse himself, his big feet literally getting in the way. All the while he became more confused and embarrassed—and all this after thinking his bride had stood him up at the altar. He was beside himself. I, on the other hand, could not stop laughing. The comedic aspect of our ceremony did not escape me. People in the audience were chuckling. Our guests appreciated the comic relief.

The whole event was hilarious. Just being around these very strict Orthodox people in this solemn, dreary little *shul* (house of worship) set me off from the beginning. The rabbi kept asking Jerry what his father's Hebrew name was in order to establish his identity for record keeping. Well, Jerry's father had died when he was young, and he didn't know the answers to some of the questions.

Later, Jerry told me he was thinking that if the marriage didn't work out, considering the rocky beginning, it could be annulled since he did not understand the languages the rabbi spoke.

Meanwhile, my other suitor, Max from Nebraska, heard that I got married. I was told that he took a plunge into depression. Although I felt bad for him, it was gratifying to hear that he cared that much.

Here I was, finally a bride, and my parents were far away in Israel. I felt so sad for my mother that she couldn't attend my wedding, the same way she had missed my sister's wedding. Also, she died just before my daughter got married. Those were important events she never got to experience.

Jerry rented a one-bedroom apartment for us in a two-story apartment building on Wilton Place in Hollywood. I was already signed up to take night classes at the University of Judaism, and during the day I continued working at the insurance office, typing up premium notices as a clerk.

One of my co-workers was Susanna, a refugee from Hungary. We became friends. She was single and decided never to marry or have children. She couldn't imagine bringing children into this world, given her life experiences as a war child. Our office supervisor was an attractive woman, slender, red-haired, and fashionably dressed. One day she shared that she was about to celebrate her twenty-fifth wedding anniversary. I remember asking her, "Twenty-five years with the same husband!?" In Israel, we had always heard that divorce was rampant in America.

She said, "Yes, we've been married for twenty-five years, and all of our friends are still married, too. Not all American couples get divorced!"

MAKING A NEST TOGETHER

Before we had been married even a year, Jerry said, "It's a shame to pay rent. Let's buy a house so we can have deductions and pay less in taxes." And I said, "Let's."

ABOVE, ERICA AND JERRY, 2008
RIGHT, IN 1960

OUR WEDDING CEREMONY,
JUNE 5, 1960

We found a house on Greenbush in Van Nuys, a suburb of Los Angeles in the San Fernando Valley. We needed one thousand dollars for the down payment. Between the two of us, we were able to come up with the money. Then we discovered that to close the deal, with points for this and points for that, we needed another thousand dollars. We didn't have it, so we went to Jerry's mother for a loan. She said, "No. If you don't have enough for the whole down payment, it's too soon to buy a house."

But if we couldn't complete the purchase of the house, we would lose the thousand-dollar down payment we already spent.

What to do? I wrote to my parents in Israel and asked if they could raise the money for us. I knew they didn't have any savings, but I asked Papa if he could borrow the money. He borrowed money from the insurance company where he worked and sent it to us. It would have been a big deal for us to lose the one thousand dollars we had already invested. My parents were always there for us. Later in life, we paid them back every penny. We were lucky that at least one side of the family was there for us when we were a young couple starting out and we needed a hand, not a handout.

I've mentioned earlier my interest in psychic phenomena. Jerry's mother shared my intrigue in the occult as well. Soon after Jerry and I were married, she told us about the Reverend Badger, a medium in the Santa Monica area who conducted séances. We decided to check him out. On the scheduled evening, we entered a big room full of people. No one spoke. Donations were made at the door. The Reverend Badger would go into a trance and move through the room from one person to another—we were sitting in a circle—bringing messages from the "Above" as they were related to him by his departed sister in the spirit world.

That night, he stopped in front of someone in the audience. "You have a daughter, and she rides horses," he said. The person he was addressing was nodding her head. "Make sure that on Sunday, the eighth, she doesn't get on a horse—to avoid an accident waiting to happen." He was very specific. I was impressed. As he continued to move around the room, he stopped in front of Jerry and said, "She can finally rest in peace. She and the baby are happy. You have finally found somebody to live your life with." Jerry's mouth dropped open. Then the Reverend Badger moved in front of me. "Oh," he exclaimed, "I smell the aroma of stuffed cabbage." One of the few things I knew how to cook was stuffed cabbage—Dita had taught me. We ate a lot of stuffed cabbage. "I see a warm home," he continued. "By the end of the year you will have an addition to your family." I was pregnant at the time with Diana and didn't know it.

Jerry was very kind and supportive, but a part of him was closed off. He would never talk about his relationship with his first wife. Hidden in the attic in the Greenbush house, I found some pictures of their wedding, which showed all the happiness and celebration. I respected his silence, and yet I wondered, when Jerry and I made love in those early years: Was he making love to me, or was she on his mind? Knowing about the divorce rate in America, I had vowed never to marry a divorced man. I thought that if you could not make it in one relationship, how would you fare in a second one?

But I never considered the situation of having a ghost from a previous marriage as competition. His first wife was a nice woman, I heard. She was lovely—pictures don't lie. She was tall; I was short. (I always wanted to be tall.) Lucky for me, after a while the "ghost" of his first wife disappeared. I got over it. I stopped obsessing. I threw myself into my new life. I was happy. I was excited. I had married a fine, handsome husband. Life was good.

We were so pleased to move into our own little house on Greenbush. The house is still there. It had 1,800 square feet with two bedrooms, one bathroom, and a good-sized backyard with a swing set. We lived there for four years, and both of our children, Diana and Johnny, were born there.

FIRST-TIME MOTHER

Our first child, Diana, arrived on February 23, 1961, at St. Joseph's Hospital in Burbank, a Catholic institution, which meant I had Jesus on the wall, facing me. I felt safe. After all, I was in America, and Jesus was part of my tribe. My pregnancy with Diana was not a picnic. It was rough. During the pregnancy, I threw up all the time, from beginning to end. Jerry often went to the corner gas station to get the car cleaned because I had thrown up in it again. Labor was difficult, and it took about two days for Diana to be born. She kicked herself out at eight months and one week. She is still kicking. She wants to live three lives in one. She weighed 7 pounds, 8 ounces—big for me. Had she been full term, I was told, and just a few ounces more, I would have needed a caesarean section.

We chose the name Diana because it means strength and justice. I wanted my daughter to be strong, and she is. The name also honors someone I admired and respected—Moshe Dayan, one of Israel's most esteemed military leaders. He was chief of staff of the Israel Defense Forces when I served in the Israeli Air Force. He was a warrior, a very strong and respected man.

Here I was, a young mother with a little tiny baby to care for. I was scared. I felt clumsy and inept. In the old country, baby holding and babysitting were reserved for grandmothers. I'd never held a baby in my arms before Diana. After she was born, Diana and I stayed at my sister's house for two weeks.

It might not be politically correct to say that motherhood was not a goal of mine. Mother Nature definitely deprived me of those supposedly wonderful feelings of being pregnant and giving birth that women are supposed to have. I never gave it much thought. Marriage and children went together. Although I did not plan for her, I'm very grateful for Diana.

I returned home with our new baby with trepidation, hoping

to live up to my new challenge of motherhood. It was a relief that Jerry was there every step of the way, including changing diapers.

Diana inherited a breathing problem from Jerry, who had asthma as a young child. When Diana was born, she was wheezing, and I was afraid she would stop breathing. But I got over those early fears as Diana began to thrive. Soon I was glad to settle into the routine a baby required.

I taught Hebrew School at Temple Maarav in Encino until a few days before Diana arrived. I resumed teaching soon after she was born and continued for the next eleven years. The few hours of teaching in the afternoon were a perfect arrangement. Jerry was at home watching over our daughter. Did I feel guilty being a working mom? Sure. I received disapproving comments all around me—from friends and family alike. "Poor Jerry!" people would say. "He has to take care of the baby by himself when she's not home."

It prompted me to do my own research to find out if homemakers were better mothers than those who worked outside the home. The data suggested that having well-adjusted children depends on many factors. The single factor of being a working mother was not a negative, in and of itself, which gave me peace of mind that I was OK. I had always insisted that you can do it all—if you have help and are organized.

Fortunately for all of us, when Diana was six months old, my parents emigrated from Israel and lived with us. Diana got a lot of holding and hugging from my mother—not from me. I was driven to pursue my career and was not bashful to ask for help from my family.

PERSUADED

Persuading my parents to immigrate to the United States is a story in and of itself. I could not bear the thought of my parents getting on in age and dying alone in Israel when their two daughters lived in America. I wrote often, urging them to come and stay. They had never met Jerry. He encouraged my efforts to bring them to America. He felt assured he could assist them in finding something to do for a living, perhaps a job in an insurance company or a dry-cleaning store, or something else.

Dita and Israel were very much against our parents emigrating. They felt that the adjustment would be too difficult. Papa and Mama were already in their fifties. They did not speak English. They had a home, family, and friends in Israel. Dita still remembered the struggle she and her husband went through when they moved to the United States and how much Israel had wanted to go back to his homeland during those early years. America was much too big for him, but Dita would not hear of it and they stayed.

So the debate raged. I continued to urge my parents to come.

I knew they could stay with us until they got on their feet. My mother had no life of her own. She lived through my father and later through me. I felt sad for her even though I did not respect her passivity. I felt strongly that I needed to persuade them to join us. When I'm convinced of something, I make a good case. I probably would have made a good lawyer, and perhaps I will be one in my next life. I thought that after all my parents had been through, they should not be separated from their daughters. I decided I wouldn't have it.

They were persuaded. They sold their place in Ramat Chen and came to Los Angeles to live with us. Diana was six months old when they arrived. My mother was in heaven. She clasped the baby to her bosom, and for the first time ever, I saw tears in her eyes. In the worst of times, I had never seen my mother cry. Now, as she held Diana in her arms, the tears flowed down her cheeks as she told me how sorry she was that she hadn't been able to hold me and show me the affection she now showed Diana.

Through her relationship with her granddaughter, my mother got in touch with her feelings of sadness and regret that she couldn't be there for me emotionally when I was a child. For me, that was deeply touching and meaningful.

Like my mother, I was not a nurturing parent, but I did the best I could at that time. It was not good enough, but you can never go back and undo your actions. What you can do is make amends and move on, as Diana and I were able to do later in life.

Diana and my mother became very attached to each other. My mother found a new purpose in life, taking care of Diana. When we three were in the same room, Diana would reach out for her rather than me. My mother became concerned when Diana ignored me and became close to her. Actually, I was relieved that my mother would pick up where I left off. I told her not to fret. I was a working mother—not a "mother-mother." "Don't you worry," I kept telling my mother. "Diana will always know who her mother is." The relationship was good for both of them and for me, too.

The adjustment to American life was difficult for my parents. I was convinced that with Jerry's positive attitude and entrepreneurship, they would be OK. I am giving Jerzry a lot of credit. Had I been married to any other man, who knows? Jerry was patient and steadfast in his mission to help my parents settle in.

Jerry took Papa all over Los Angeles to look for work. They found a German-speaking import/export company, and Papa was hired to man the phones. When he got nervous, it was like he became deaf. He couldn't hear. "Hello, who is this? Hello? Hello?" His first job ended before long. The beat went on. They checked out various positions at insurance companies, but the language barrier was too great. The search for a job stretched out over many months.

Papa became so depressed that he wouldn't get out of bed. After being a highly functioning senior executive at Zion Insurance Company in Israel, with forty employees working for him, he could not find or hold a job. Jerry suggested opening a dry-cleaning store.

At first, my father was very offended. He felt he was being asked to be like a *schneider* (a tailor)—the lowest position on the totem pole of professions, perhaps one notch above a shoemaker. He was European, after all, and what you did for a living mattered! His self-esteem took a beating. Eventually he agreed with Jerry that a cleaning business wasn't a bad idea, and my mother could get involved as well. Papa realized that beggars can't be choosers.

A license was needed to operate a dry-cleaning and laundry establishment. Jerry (who else?) would have to be the licensee. Jerry is very smart, but he has two left hands (he's not good at repairs) and two left feet (in dancing). And he had never ironed a garment in his life. But somehow he demonstrated that he had the skills to operate a cleaning business and got himself a license.

We opened the first dry-cleaning store in North Hollywood, on Riverside Drive across from the Diplomat Hotel. We took in clothes and sent them out to a plant to be cleaned. How do you get clientele? Jerry decided to go door-to-door and pick up clothes.

I can delegate and run businesses, but I can't do face-to-face marketing. I refused to knock on doors. It spooked me. How do you know who's behind the door? Jerry would be the one to knock on the door, and I would hide in the bushes. It was funny.

People opened their doors and gave Jerry their linens. They would ask, "How much is a panel?" At first we didn't have a clue what a panel was. They were trying to get prices on drapes. Jerry would say, "Just a moment. I'll check." He called my father.

"How much do we charge for a panel?"

My father replied, "What's a panel?"

Then Jerry would make up a price and they would hand over their items to be cleaned. Thanks to Jerry's efforts, business began to take off. We simply went door-to-door in the neighborhood and recruited new customers by picking up dirty laundry. It is amazing what people will give you. They trusted us with their dirty treasures. Trusting strangers was a foreign concept for me then and is to this day.

Soon after opening the dry-cleaning store, my parents began to take in tailoring as well. At last, my father saw that he could earn a living. After a few months, they got their own place and moved out of our home. Papa liked being his own boss. Even as an insurance underwriter, he had to answer to the president of the company. Now he was the "president." And guess what—he loved the ladies. Since my mother worked in the store, she watched him like a hawk. When he would get home from delivering dry-cleaned clothes she would question, "How come it took you so long?" My father would protest, "I was gone just a few minutes; what could I have done in a few minutes?"

A year or so passed. My parents made a living and we were all happy to be together. Life was good. One day Jerry said to Papa, "It is time to open a bigger store in Hollywood," and they did. My parents also moved to larger quarters in an apartment complex nearby. They moved up in the world.

Across from their apartment was a movie house called the Pussycat. One day Papa said to Mama, "Let's go to the movies." They went in and the flick began. Suddenly my mother realized what it was—an adult movie of the kind she had never been privy to.

"Mendel," she demanded hurriedly, "let's go."

He sheepishly replied, "Why?"

Mother dragged him out.

OUR GROWING FAMILY

Johnny was born on June 22, 1964, three and a half years after Diana. The pregnancy was easy. He came out smiling. This little baby always smiled. We named him Robert John, after Jerry's grandmother Rachel and his uncle John, both of whom had passed away. We started calling the baby Johnny. As an adult, Johnny officially changed his name to John Robert Miller.

Diana welcomed Johnny's arrival. He was so cute, and everyone oohed and aahed over him. She adopted an important role in the family, mothering and protecting her little brother. She would not leave his side. In grade school, she was always dragging him

WITH OMAMA AND OPAPA ON GREENBUSH AVENUE,
VAN NUYS, 1962

FUN AT THE BEACH, 1963

9756 AQUEDUCT STREET, SEPULVEDA, 1967

WITH OUR TEENAGERS, 1976

along with her, and she got attention when he was with her. Her friends used to blame me for making her babysit her brother all the time. I never did. She always wanted him. She guided him all along: This is the teacher you should have; these are the classes you should take. In my opinion, the reason he went to law school was because she went to law school.

After they grew up, we played family games and the question came up, "Who was the most influential person in your life?" To my surprise Johnny would say, "My sister." I thought it was me. They are still very close. They talk all the time and see each other often. It makes me feel wonderful.

I continued teaching Hebrew school after my parents moved out of our home. I hired neighborhood high school kids as babysitters. Both Diana and Johnny were given chores early in life. I figured out that it was too much for me to do it all by myself. I decided that our home was not a hotel or restaurant. We did not have a maid, so everybody had to help. As young children, each had their own clothes hamper and did their own laundry. They helped clean. They made their own lunches. They liked complaining to their friends about all the work they had to do at home. But I did well. Both of our children grew up to be competent and self-reliant, an outcome of early responsibilities. I do not know where I got the wisdom to demand help from my family. This was unheard of among my peers.

Diana used to complain to me, "You're not a good mom." I

replied, "If you don't like it, get adopted. Find another mother." In Diana's eyes, I didn't measure up. As I pursued my career goals, I wasn't the mother who spent time baking cookies. I wasn't there for her the way other mothers were there for their children. In retrospect, Diana's complaints were valid on most counts. I fell short on being the mother she needed me to be.

In my defense, though, I was a dutiful mother. I did what I had to do to keep her safe. I provided order and structure in her daily existence even though she missed out on a doting, affectionate mother, which I was able to be three years later with Johnny.

I did not breastfeed either of my children but propped the bottle in their mouths, going about my business in lieu of holding and cuddling. I am so sorry. I did not know any better. I did not have the information then about how important it is to cuddle and rock newborn babies.

On the positive side, I must note that in spite of my busy schedule, my family was always very important to me. I did not neglect them. I made sure we spent time together. We had frequent family functions along with many outings and trips. We saw my parents every weekend. I am so glad that we did.

Every Sunday, they came for dinner and stayed overnight. Every Friday evening, they spent time with my sister. During the week, my mother would sit by the phone and wait for me to call. She used to complain to my sister that I didn't call her enough. She was very disappointed with me, just as she became disappointed with my father when he stopped reading to her and engaging her in daily conversations.

When they lived in our house, she would sit up and wait until I got home so she could hear about my daily activities. She wanted to know details about my work and my friends. She asked a lot of questions such as, "What did he say, what did she say?" I did not appreciate her neediness, but I tried to answer all her questions because I felt sorry for her. It felt like a burden, but I did it anyway.

We included my parents in most of our activities: going to the beach, sightseeing, and going on vacations. Very little gave my mother pleasure except being with her family. I so much wanted to make her happy, to do things for her, but she needed nothing. She exemplified the meaning of anhedonia, the inability to enjoy pleasure in life, any pleasure at all.

According to my mother, my father was a philanderer. He fooled around all during their marriage. My father strongly objected to her allegations and swore on his life that my mother's imagination made up all of those stories. I tuned them both out, thinking they were both half right. No child, no matter how old, wants to hear about his or her parents' sex life or lack thereof.

The first time I was exposed firsthand to my father's indiscretions was when our children were toddlers and our young housekeeper, Esmeralda, said to me one day, "Oh, oh, here comes your father. I will have to go to my room and hide."

"Why?" I asked, dumbfounded.

"I did not want to tell you," she replied. "Your father is a really nice man, but every time he visits and I am alone in the kitchen, he tries to feel me up."

"Sorry, Esmeralda," I told her. "I did not know. Go ahead and avoid him whenever he visits us." In my thinking, she was an adult. In Rumania, it was common for servants to be used sexually, and I never made a big deal about it.

Later in life, when my parents retired from the dry-cleaning business, my father worked part-time in Jerry's office. One day Jerry's secretary told him that my father made unwanted advances toward her. Her objection was not that he did so but that he was a married man. She threatened to quit, and Jerry had no option but to let my father go. Jerry had a series of secretaries who had quit on him while my father was working in his office, and until this one came forward, he could never figure out why.

The family, especially my mother, was very upset that Jerry had fired my father. We could not tell her the reason. We wanted to spare her the truth.

When Diana was about eleven, she had a good friend next door. One day the friend's mother said to me, "Erica, I want to tell you that my Susie came to me and told me that your father put his hand under her shirt. Susie's friend Alane is the daughter of a police officer. If he messes with Alane, she will tell her dad, and your father will end up in jail. He will be registered as a sex offender and marked for life."

I freaked. To mess with adults is one thing—they can fend for themselves. But messing with children is a whole different ball-game. I called my sister and asked her whether Papa had ever messed with us girls, and she said, "Never!"

The next time Papa came to the house, I took him outside in the backyard. He knew immediately that I was upset. I had heard about the servant and the secretary. Even as a young child, I had heard that Papa fooled around with Aunt Berta in the compound. But this was the first time I had heard about Papa and children.

I said, "Papa, Rachel next door told me that you fondled Susie. I can only tell you that if I ever hear again that you touched any children, not only will you never come to our house again, I'll never let you see the children, and yes, I will have nothing to do with you, ever. Do you hear me? Lay off the children!"

He looked at me and knew I was serious and meant what I said. He did not deny anything, nor did he apologize. The only thing he said was, "Don't tell Mama."

Then I asked Diana if my father had ever touched her inappropriately. She said, "Yes, but I kind of avoid him." I asked Johnny, who was eight at that time, "Did Opapa ever try to touch you or fondle you?" He said, "Yeah."

After I confronted my father, I never heard of any further incidents with children. I addressed the issue up-front with my kids, and life went on. He was my father, after all. I loved him.

My sister had difficulty forgiving him. He had messed with her children as well. She wasn't able to talk to him for many months after she found out. Her children, just like mine, never told on my father. He was their grandfather! They couldn't, they wouldn't!

BACK TO SCHOOL

When Johnny was in first grade, I went back to college. The year was 1970 and I was thirty-six. I began taking classes at a community college on Fulton in North Hollywood. During the first year, my English instructor, Mr. Jones, used four-letter words throughout his lectures. I think he was into shock value. Certainly European or Israeli professors would never treat language with such disrespect. But he was a good teacher and the students liked him. Jerry thought he shouldn't be in the classroom. But Professor Jones was OK in my book. I earned an A in English 101. Jerry couldn't believe it. Although he was a good student and a natural-born American, he never received an A in English. Meanwhile, he continued to be bothered by my reports of profanity in the classroom.

Finally I told Jerry, "You're a bag of wind. If you don't like it, try to have him fired." Jerry took up the challenge. He decided to run for office on the board of the community college district so he might be instrumental in firing Professor Jones. Jerry traveled around Northridge—a suburb of Los Angeles—and collected signatures to get on the ballot. He didn't win election to the board, but he did get a lot of votes. Jerry Brown, the son of the former governor of California, was also running for office at the time, so we often joked about the "Jerry" candidates.

I didn't know if I could make it as a college student, with a husband and children to care for, but when I got an A in English, I said to myself, "OK, let's see how far I can go." After I completed my associate in arts degree, I enrolled in California State University–Northridge, and in 1974 I received a bachelor of arts in general education with an emphasis in psychology.

During my eleven years as a Hebrew teacher to that point, I had encountered many children with emotional and behavioral problems. I had frequent meetings with their parents. Sometimes the causes of their problems were obvious to me, and other times they were not. I wanted to understand what makes children and parents tick. I decided to go back to school and become a psychologist. This was a highly momentous decision for our family's future.

I studied hard. Academics didn't come easily to me. In addition to my studies, I was still teaching Hebrew school, so I had to be super organized. I was conscientious about cooking and taking care of my family as well. On Sundays, when my colleagues were going to growth groups and social events, I stayed home and cooked for the week, making packages of food for Jerry and the kids. The kids did fine. Between my mother and Jerry, they were in good hands.

My dream of going to medical school was out of reach for me. With children and a husband who was less than enthusiastic about me playing my own fiddle, becoming a psychologist was a good alternative. Although he never said so, I am positive Jerry would have liked a wife who walked one step behind him, just like his mama did with her husband. It was not to be. I was driven to push my limits.

I didn't get involved in campus activities like most of my colleagues. For me it was go to class and return home. I had no time or interest in socializing. I had but one friend and fellow conspirator. Her name was Meryl. She was a married woman with two children, and like me, she aspired to become a psychologist. We commiserated and studied together, and we shared a dream about becoming psychologists and opening a combined private practice.

She was sensitive, bright, and a free spirit. She also was bisexual. The first time I was exposed to bisexuality and lesbianism was in the Israeli Air Force. Then, I didn't even know what that meant. The rumor was that two women in our unit were "together." I recall that the authorities split them up and eventually expelled them from the base. I am glad that this is no longer the case. People's sexuality is a private and personal matter.

When I studied with Meryl in her home, I found her odd but rather interesting. She would go swimming nude in her pool and seemed completely uninhibited. Once when I said good night, she kissed me on the mouth. After that time, I avoided good-byes, and she got the message. I told Jerry about my unexpected, weird experience. It was the first and only time a woman went for my mouth. Lucky for me, I was not homophobic, and I shrugged it off. She did not impose her adventurous nature on me further.

She told me she was seeing a therapist who encouraged her to experience herself in every possible way. She also had a boyfriend. She and her husband both were swingers. I'm relieved I never had the desire to experiment in the fast lane of drugs and extramarital sex. The implications and consequences kept me in check.

Despite our big plans to set up a mental health clinic, our dream of sharing a private practice was not to be. I was very disappointed when Meryl disappeared suddenly and dropped out of school and my life. Later, I heard that she had divorced her husband and moved out of the area with her boyfriend. She never informed me of her whereabouts. My defense mechanism of detachment came in handy then, as it always does. Losses and disappointments are part of life. I shrugged my shoulders and moved on.

Statistics was a requirement for obtaining a degree in psychology, and it was a very difficult subject for me. As an undergraduate student at California State, I asked for assistance, and they assigned me a tutor. This nice young man looked at me and inquired curiously, "Are you Mrs. Miller?" He had been one of my students at Temple Maarav Hebrew School. Now it was his turn to help me, and I gratefully passed statistics. Life is an amazing journey. Often what goes around comes around.

I had moments in which dividing my time between home and school was more than I could bear, yet I never wavered from my plan to go to graduate school. I thought I could make it but was not sure. I definitely knew I wanted to become a psychologist. My plan was to get a doctorate and do clinical work.

Just as with the Air Force and the tourist office, I knew exactly the school for me: the California School of Professional Psychology (CSPP) in Los Angeles. I didn't even apply to USC or UCLA. I didn't want to do research. I wanted practical training for clinical work. After several interviews, I was accepted into the program. I did it! I got in!

CALIFORNIA SCHOOL OF PROFESSIONAL PSYCHOLOGY (CSPP)

Graduate school was my biggest challenge yet. The demands and pressures of being a graduate student and homemaker were almost insurmountable. I had little, if any, support at home. Nobody wanted me to become a graduate student.

My mother was ambivalent at best. She was afraid that Jerry would stray and find another woman. "You know how men are," she warned. Everyone in the family was against my decision, including Jerry's mother. The comments included criticism about returning to school "at your age!"

"*Poor Jerry*," everyone thought. It didn't seem to matter that I continued my domestic tasks, cooking the meals and taking care of many household duties. Jerry allowed himself to be a victim. He wanted me to be at his side, like a shadow, and promote him so he would be the one in the limelight. In his defense, he never bargained for the driven wife I turned out to be. His cousin, Neil, would say, "She's going to run away with one of those crazy psychiatrists. Send her back to Rumania!"

I felt alone, so alone. I had no support for my ambitious endeavor. As in the past, I did what I had to do. I went for it. I walked to the beat of my own drum without approval from my family. No one could stop me!

Classes were held in the evening. Jerry would ask me repeatedly, "Do you have to go out again tonight?" I would reply, "I'm not doing anything wrong. I'm not gallivanting. It's not against you. It's for me."

In a sense, I was an absentee parent, and Jerry became the mother hen. He went to teachers' conferences and ran errands for the kids and took very good care of them. While I was in graduate school, that's the way it had to be. I did what I could to help. The family became tired of the food I prepared for them on Sundays. Unbeknownst to me, they would often get fast food instead. It felt like them versus me, but that was the price. We all sacrificed.

Many married women attended CSPP, and a lot of marriages broke up. With mothers studying full time, there are horrendous stressors on the family. Professors don't care whether you have a family or not—you are responsible for all of the assignments. Once I realized I had the ability to do the work, I couldn't be stopped. If Jerry had acted on his wishes—that is, had he really put pressure on me to drop the program—I would have had to leave the marriage. I was determined to get my PhD!

From Jerry's perspective:

The only really tough times for Erica and me were during the years she was a full-time student in pursuit of her PhD and our children were young. Erica wanted to go back to school, and we had a family. She was driven to get her PhD, and it was important to her. She was very determined. There was no stopping her. She did not miss a beat: four years undergraduate, two years for her master's, two years for her PhD. It was tough for all of us. I became the mother hen. I went to parent-teacher conferences. I did what I had to do, filling in for Erica whenever she was not available. It was definitely a family affair. We survived the challenge and prospered. I must note that despite her demanding graduate work, she made sure we knew that family was important. We always had dinner together. Sunday was family day with grandparents, and every year we took vacations with and without our children. Those were cherished times for all of us.

In graduate school, my first-year internship placement was in a school for learning-challenged and behaviorally challenged students, ages nine to eleven. In the early 1970s there wasn't as much sensitivity to learning disabilities caused by attention deficit disorder and other chemical and perceptual conditions, such as dyslexia. Educational testing and evaluation were infrequent. These were smart kids, but having been told for years that they were slow or stupid, they were already in trouble and had severe behavior problems.

In the second year of graduate school, I was placed at a mental health center in West Los Angeles, where I was able to observe and later co-lead therapy groups composed of normal neurotics in pursuit of "happiness."

My third and fourth years I interned at UCLA in west Los Angeles and Metropolitan State Hospital's psychiatric ward in Norwalk, consecutively. My experiences in those two institutions were very valuable, as I will address later.

At CSPP our performance was not evaluated according to multiple choice questions or essays, as was customary in most other graduate programs. Rather, each student was evaluated periodically by the faculty. If you did not measure up, you were given an "NS" (not sufficient). Two NS's on your record and you were out of the program. Since the evaluations were subjective, if a professor did not like you, you were toast.

My style of saying what I think, which I had internalized from my years in Israel, got me into trouble, and I almost flunked out of the program.

I had some problems with a professor who taught Rogerian theory. I don't remember exactly what the issue was, but I expressed my opinion. She said she didn't want my opinion. What she wanted was for me to spit back exactly what Rogerian theory is, and my opinion didn't matter.

By the time I realized she meant what she said, it was too late. I had treated her like an equal, like a peer, trying to have a dialogue about the issue. Apparently she was offended. In the evaluation, she gave me an NS.

During my third year of graduate school, I interned at UCLA in the Department of Legal Psychiatry—a most enviable and desirable placement. The psychiatrist in charge was a short, skinny little guy, originally from South America. Rumor had it that every year he would find a scapegoat among the interns. He would target a student who was intimidated by him.

Staff meetings were once a week. Every Friday we gathered with other interns, psychiatrists, social workers, and team members to discuss difficult cases—court-referred cases regarding domestic violence, sex offenders, child pornography, and child custody.

Case in point: The police used to pick up gay people in bath-houses and charge them with various offenses. I was part of a team that interviewed hundreds of gay men. We were to assess whether these men posed a threat to children. Back then, the stereotype was that gay men were pedophiles. Following my assessments, I would write up my observations, sign my name alongside that of a supervising psychiatrist, and send the report with our finding and recommendations to the court. The first quarter, I had a supervisor, Dr. Jennings, who complimented me in his report with comments like, "She has excellent clinical skills. She is intuitive and sensitive." The second quarter he gave me the same positive evaluation.

By the third and fourth quarters, my immediate supervisor was the psychiatrist in charge. That semester, I was the scapegoat. He made mincemeat out of me. At staff meetings when I reported on a case, he came after me. He would become irate and hammer me: "I can't understand you! Why do you still have an accent?! Why do you hang on to it? I cannot understand what you are saying."

He said this in front of the entire team. It was clearly a case of antipathy. He could not stand me. I must have reminded him of someone he disliked. For me, he became a Nazi; he was my Nazi. *He'll get me, and then I will be kicked out of the program*, I thought.

I was frantic. I went to a speech pathologist at UCLA to get rid of my accent. She told me there was nothing the matter with my verbal expression. She could understand me just fine, and getting rid of an accent takes a long time! I decided to forego the process. Back at staff meetings, my persecutor continued, "Why don't you go home and take care of your kids and your husband?"

From his perspective, I was a nebbish, a pathetic little thing. How could I sit in front of clients and be a doctor? My colleagues tried to reassure me and prep me for these meetings: "Come on, Erica, just think of him as this skinny little guy with a skinny little penis! He is probably impotent in bed and asserts all of his power putting down interns. Don't let him. Straighten up, speak up, and don't let him intimidate you."

I heard what they said but could not act on their advice. In those weekly meetings, I was literally cowering, and he saw what I projected—a little wimp. In a way, when I think about that experience, I realize that it helped me grow. No Nazi will ever get me again.

I clearly projected onto him my fears of yesterday. I saw that when he tried to put down someone else, that intern was able to respond with, "This is not helpful," or, "Wait a minute, let's get back to the issues." In retrospect, I can see that I did not stand up for myself. I couldn't. I was immobilized.

He kept on beating me down, and I was unable to respond on the spot, which was clearly due to the baggage of my early years.

Then, the unthinkable happened. At the end of the third year of training, my supervisor gave me an NS. I now had two NS's on my record. I would be dropped from the program.

I was crushed. At CSPP, everyone talked about me: "She's going to be thrown out." I saw myself as a marked person. All during those long weeks, I wanted to disappear, become invisible. I was an "it." Once again, I was the only little Jewish girl in the Catholic school, looking around to see who else didn't wear a cross. I felt exposed and vulnerable—vulnerable like never before—but I did not go away.

In the concentration camp, my mother had been there and sheltered me from evil. In the Israeli Air Force, while at war, I had felt the protection of the other soldiers. At CSPP, when expelled, I was all alone. I panicked. I wanted to slink into a corner and suck my thumb. I didn't want to face my persecutors. There was no one to come to my rescue. I thought about all the sacrifices I had made and all that we had gone through as a family. I never actually doubted my competence, but my insecurities about my *safety* were triggered. *They're going to get me. The system is going to get me.*

I had done my best, yet life owed me nothing. There are forces in life beyond my control. Yet, I could not let this happen. This development was not acceptable to me. Many others would have given up at this point—you don't take on City Hall, or a university. But I could not quit. I would not quit.

I would not be stopped. Just like my mother before me, in times of crises I found a core of inner strength. I went into high gear. I hired an attorney. I threatened to sue CSPP. I took on CSPP, Legal Psychiatry, and the big chief. Of course, CSPP stood up for one of its own, as they wanted to keep their internship placement at UCLA for their students. Everybody wanted me to vanish, disappear, go away, but I couldn't, I wouldn't. For two or three months, my fate hung in the balance.

I refused to leave the school until my hearing. I continued attending classes. Everyone was aware of my case. It was all over the school. Students avoided me like the plague. When I walked down the hallways, my colleagues glanced at me and quickly looked away. Other students felt threatened, I'm sure. I was an example of what could happen to them. Everyone was subject to the tremendous pressure of grades and evaluations coupled with the uncomfortable, often unhealthy, and arbitrary authoritarian power structure of the school.

I felt terribly isolated during a time when I really needed support. It was a dreadful situation. I was devastated but absolutely determined not to go under. I believe that where there is life, there is hope. My lifelong resolve and determination came to my rescue once more. I was a survivor!

At the hearings at CSPP, with my lawyer at my side, I was detached, very detached. I felt no emotions. I dared not breathe. At one end of the room the school authorities were sitting at a table. On the other side, I sat with my attorney and my witnesses. A few colleagues came to testify for me. They did not look the other way. In the face of injustice, they got involved. I give them a lot of credit. Each one was taking a risk of becoming persona non grata.

My witnesses attested to my clinical skills and their view of me as a competent colleague. They said the problem had to be a personality difference.

My attorney pointed out that you could not be praised as a fine clinician for two quarters by one psychiatrist and then suddenly become totally incompetent. We made my case. With my very visible attorney, CSPP had a public lawsuit staring them in the face. While they didn't want to offend UCLA's Department of Legal Psychiatry, they didn't want to take a position that wouldn't hold up in court, based on the evidence. I was reinstated! I know now that if I had hesitated, if I had not engaged an attorney quickly, I would have been out.

Although severely shaken, I was on my feet and running. My fourth and final year of internship was at Metropolitan State Hospital in Norwalk, and it was a wonderful training ground. The three-hour round-trip to Norwalk every day was brutal. So? You do what you have to do.

Coming home on the 405 freeway, I would struggle to stay awake, but the rewards were worth it. I worked with psychotic, depressed, and suicidal patients, on both an inpatient and outpatient basis. I felt very competent as I discovered I could really relate to this pathological population, the people who heard voices and had difficulty distinguishing between fantasy and reality. I helped run therapy groups for very bright college-age kids who suffered from a first psychotic break, as well as their parents—moms and dads trying to deal with their children's mental illness, which would be a lifelong struggle.

It prepared me for working with the severely mentally ill. It was a wonderful, rewarding final year. I would be graduating, I would be moving on. I would achieve my goal. I would have a PhD after my name, and no one would ever be able to take it away!

In the process of regaining my confidence regarding my clinical abilities, luck had it that during the last year of my graduate program, I had a tutorial with the first president of CSPP, Dr. Arthur Kovacs. The tutorial required me to act as a supervisor to an intern from a lower grade, asking questions and giving feedback on an ongoing case study. The meetings were tape-recorded so that Dr. Kovacs could critique my clinical supervisory skills.

On a weekly basis for a whole semester, I would go to the home of Dr. Kovacs on Poinsettia, near Fairfax, for the review sessions. Even though I felt competent, I was still easily intimidated. I had almost flunked out of school, but the tutorial with Dr. Kovacs made a big difference!

Oh, did I have a crush on Dr. Kovacs! That tutorial was thrilling and intimidating—like being in a fishbowl, naked and exposed every week. If I had any doubts about my clinical skills; that I was a natural; that I was intuitive, sensitive, and well trained, they evaporated. Dr. Kovacs would exclaim, "Yes. Yes. Exactly right. I couldn't have made a better interpretation myself! Someday you will make a wonderful supervisor." I felt empowered, and my

COVER OF MY DISSERTATION

confidence in being a good clinician resurged. So my last year in graduate school was good, very good.

My dissertation committee liked my work. The topic was close to my heart. As a liberated female, I wondered about and researched gender issues. My dissertation title was, "Sex Identity, Sex Concepts, and Personality Adjustment in Three Generations of Males." I had a son and a husband, males on two parts of the age spectrum. I was interested in the impact of women's liberation on the male psyche of different generations. Who fared best, the young or the older?

Writing a thesis presented more obstacles. I don't have trouble with verbal expression, but the statistical aspect of research was difficult for me. I had to have help with statistical interpretations of my findings. Someone recommended a female statistician from Topanga Canyon. I gave her my data and told her about the deadline. Weeks went by. I didn't hear from her and I couldn't reach her. I began to get frantic. I didn't know how to get my material back. She didn't return my calls. I almost missed the deadline. It turned out that her partner had beaten her up, and she had to go into hiding. Finally, we connected, and I did make the deadline. It had been a final nightmare.

No matter what lessons life teaches me, I will always try to be in control as much as I can. I will avoid situations in which I must depend on someone else. I am very competent. I clean my house much better than my cleaning crew, trust me. So if they don't show up, it's no big deal. I can handle it. I can do it myself. In running my businesses, I delegate, supervise, and oversee—very hands-on. My policy is, "Trust, but always verify."

The drama of my four years in graduate school was over. I received wonderful clinical training and was strengthened by personal trauma. Since then, I have never set foot in CSPP, nor even gone near the campus. I haven't kept in contact with alumni. It was simply too traumatic. In those years, CSPP was a zoo, and very unstructured, too. The hierarchy consisted of typical egocentric, power-driven administrative personalities. I'm sure I wasn't the only vulnerable student who suffered. I understand that things have since improved.

At my graduation, my family had a big celebration. There I was with my PhD diploma and my cap and gown—and with my parents and family around me. We all hung in there together. As Hillary Clinton once said, "It takes a village." We made it! I was so very grateful.

LAST YEARS WITH MY PARENTS

Toward the end of my parents' lives, we had some wonderful times together. All of us would pile into the car along with Mama and Papa, and we would drive to the beach. My mother got carsick very quickly, just like I did.

One time, on our evening return from the beach, Mama was

ON THE OCCASION OF MY PHD IN CLINICAL PSYCHOLOGY,
1978, WITH JOHNNY, JERRY, AND DIANA

WITH PAPA, DITA, AND MAMA

sitting in the backseat next to the kids. She informed us that she was motion sick. The routine was that Jerry would give her a bucket. She would throw up. We would stop the car, and she would leave the bucket outside by the road. This time, as we drove off again, Diana said, "Omama, where are your teeth?" She had lost them in the bucket. We drove back in the dark to look for the bucket, but we never found it or her teeth.

The following day, my mother had a meeting with the German consulate to work out Holocaust reparations. Reparations were given to those whose lives had been disrupted by the Nazis. They would receive a stipend of two hundred to three hundred dollars monthly for the rest of their lives. The process required Mama to visit a German psychiatrist to assess the extent to which she was damaged.

Having lost her teeth in the bucket the day before, she was mumbling her words. The psychiatrist took one look at her and said, "That's good enough. You're eligible." From that time on, she received a small pension for having been incarcerated for four years. My sister receives reparation money as well. I, on the other hand, was not eligible, because I could not show financial hardship. You would think that four years of incarceration would suffice for monetary reparation.

My father died in the late 1970s. He was 80. He simply dropped dead. His end was quick, and he did not suffer. My mother died in

DITA AND ME AT OUR PARENTS GRAVESTONES, FORREST LAWN,
BURBANK, CALIFORNIA

the early 1980s. She was 80 and went quickly as well. I am grateful on both accounts.

When my father died, I requested an open casket. I was determined to stare willfully and defiantly into the face of death. When I saw his lifeless body lying there, all made up like a grotesque mannequin, I went to pieces. It brought my cumulative pain of loss to the surface. I cried for my friend Aaron and all the dead people I had seen during the war. I cried for the unspeakable humiliation and cruelty toward my father that I had witnessed. I cried and sobbed with absolutely no shame. It seemed that the flood of my tears would never stop.

This was the closest I came to an out-of-body experience. I watched myself wail and thought clearly, "The cruelty of the human condition. You strive, you achieve, and in one split second you're a corpse. The banality of life—last night I saw Papa. He was alive. I said 'good-bye.' Today he is a lifeless cadaver."

Such a display of grief was out of character for me. My father's death opened the floodgates of years of pent-up grief.

JERRY

Jerry, I'm proud to say, is my life partner. He figures prominently throughout this memoir. He has been solidly by my side all through our married life. It does not matter, it really does not matter, that he was less than enthusiastic during my graduate school saga. He stuck by me through thick and thin. That's what matters.

Jerry is an idea man and a skillful "marketer." He can sell a pet rock. Consider how he established a cleaning business for my parents. I always encouraged and applauded this quality.

With my encouragement, over the years Jerry evolved and became an entrepreneur. He bought and sold several businesses, always at a profit. At the same time, he invested in income properties. He did well for us. I am a good wife for Jerry. We complement each other. We have led independent lives in some areas, separate, but together. We are unusual in our peer group. Decisions about spending money, what to do next, setting our priorities—I am always an active participant. There is no head of our household. We are equal partners with all the rights and responsibilities.

Despite the traditional American way of the man being the wage earner and financial decision maker, we have worked out a good partnership. To the amusement of many, I have my own checking account. He has his. I have my own money-market fund. He has his. When we go out to eat, he pays. I buy the groceries. We don't squabble about money. When I want to go on a trip, don't tell me we can't afford it. I pay half and he pays half.

Jerry's mother was fearful and obsessed about money. She kept Jerry and his father down and used to blame her husband for failures. Jerry's father was a very nice man who died at the age of fifty-two. When Jerry married me, he was afraid I was going to say, "Don't try. You might fail." I continually reminded him, "I'm not your mother." I always applauded his ideas and risk taking.

In the early years of our marriage, I tried to have Israeli friends and to stay in touch with Israel. But Israelis in America were very clannish. When we got together, they always spoke Hebrew. They didn't mean to be exclusive, but anyone who didn't understand Hebrew was completely left out. I felt very protective of Jerry, so eventually we stopped getting together with Israelis. We never did develop Israeli friends. It just didn't work out. All of our social groups came through Jerry's contacts.

When we lived on Greenbush, my sister and I inherited a four-plex. Jerry always had a vision—like the game Monopoly. If you buy a property and then take the profits and buy something else, you increase the number of units. That's how we increased our family's assets. Today, we are the proud owners of twelve apartment buildings in Los Angeles and Austin, Texas, exceeding 200 units. I am very proud of our achievements.

At this stage of our marriage I feel closer to Jerry than I ever have. We have been married more than fifty years. He is my partner, and I am very devoted to him. We enjoy our lives. We are never bored. We have animated conversations about world affairs, politics, and our children. He works in his office and I in mine, and we enjoy the time we have together. Also, we are very fortunate that we get to travel all over the world together, with our friends and once a year with our children and grandchildren—all eleven of us! In short, we have a dream of a life.

THE CHILDREN: DIANA AND JOHNNY

Diana, like me, has always marched to the beat of her own drum. It started even before she was born. Regardless of my readiness, Diana—restless, floating in the constricted area of my amniotic fluid—broke the water and freed herself after eighteen hours of struggle, three weeks before the due date.

To my dismay, over time Diana became daddy's little girl— they were too enmeshed, I thought. It did not take long for Diana to figure out that her dad could not say no to her, and she played one parent successfully against the other—the other being me. I was the disciplinarian. I set limits. I was the witch. Jerry was the prince, the protector, the one without boundaries, always ready to come to her rescue.

Jerry never fully grasped the concept of setting limits. He would often say "yes," and I would say "no way."

"You're sick? You cannot go to school?" Jerry would say. "OK, stay home." And I would say, "Unless you're dying, you must go to school."

Caught between those two extremes, Diana naturally had some issues in maturation. Yet she was an adorable, bright, and spirited child with a mind of her own—a definite challenge to my autocratic, "do as I say" parenting style. Jerry was definitely the favorite parent.

During those early years, I was frequently angry at Jerry for siding with the children and undermining my efforts to provide structure and order. I raised my voice and screamed at him often in frustration. I felt alone: me on one side, the three of them on the other. It was tough for all of us, very tough.

I am sure that the trauma of the camp during my formative years had an limiting effect on my positive interaction with my children (and later my grandchildren). I have difficulty being playful. I missed the experience of being a kid, so I have less patience and tolerance for kids than many other women. I never played with dolls like most little girls. I was impatient with my children, especially Diana, when they were young.

I used to say to Diana, "Grow up already. Be more mature!"— and she was just a child. She was not only spirited but also hyperactive. She had so much energy. She wanted this, that, and everything. She had a mind of her own. In a way, I was the same inside, but I kept it in check. I could not tolerate or support Diana's natural exuberance. I was not a competent parent in that regard.

Because of the parenting I received, my early childhood experiences, and my autocratic parenting style, Diana's and my personalities were not synchronized. Indeed, we marched to very different drums. When I needed her to sleep or eat, she wasn't tired or hungry. She wouldn't wear the frilly dresses I chose for her. She would threaten to run away. I suggested I would help her pack. She didn't measure up. Neither did I. We were at odds.

I understand that at Stephen S. Wise Temple in Los Angeles, they now have "Mommy and Me" classes especially for mothers and babies who are not synchronized, who have different rhythms. It's the adults who are responsible for getting the necessary information for competent parenting. Infants and children are helpless. They are who they are.

In family pictures, everyone is smiling. It couldn't have been all bad. But I wish I could have been a doting mother. I wish I could have made Diana feel accepted and cherished. Our lack of synchronicity made me feel out of control—a most unnerving feeling then and still now. As I analyze it today, "out of control" means extreme, heightened vulnerability second only to death. It means having no power. Is that irrational? Of course it is!

Johnny, on the other hand, had an easier time growing up than Diana. He often smiled. He was my easy child and got the best of my mothering. When he was six months old, we moved to Aqueduct Avenue in Sepulveda, and we lived there until Johnny was in the last year of junior high. He was a charmer. Cute girls were always following him around. He was in the school marching band playing the saxophone, and he took piano lessons as well. He did not mind postponing gratification as long as he reaped the rewards of being applauded after the band competitions and piano recitals.

If Diana was Jerry's little girl, Johnny was my little boy, or at least I thought he was. He definitely preferred me. Fearing that Johnny might become a mama's boy, I purposefully pushed him away so he could find his father, and he did.

Being surrounded by Jewish people was important to me. There is safety in numbers. Before we purchased our home in Sepulveda, we made sure that some of our neighbors had mezuzahs (Jewish scrolls containing the Ten Commandments) displayed on their doors, and we found quite a few.

By the time our children were looking for neighborhood play-mates, many of the Jewish families had moved away. In Sepulveda, to my dismay, we encountered anti-Semitism. The elementary school was within walking distance from our house. While walking home from school, some children accosted Diana and Johnny because they were Jewish. They took it in stride, more or less, and I overreacted. I had the school keep the bullies behind so our children could make it home safely.

Otherwise, Sepulveda was an OK place. We had the nicest home in the neighborhood—a two-story colonial house. In general, we had many good years there as our children grew up.

Although my being a full-time graduate student provided a challenge for the family, I would be remiss if I did not mention that a lot of things were right. We were and are an involved, close-knit family. We enjoyed family holidays and parties. Money wasn't plentiful, but travel was a priority.

DIANA'S WEDDING

Our kids were very well traveled. I saved the money I made as a Hebrew school teacher for the purpose of family travel. Every year we took sightseeing trips around the country—to the Rocky Mountains, Bryce Canyon National Park, and Yosemite. We went to Europe, Asia, the Middle East, Hawaii, Barbados, and Canada. Those trips were some of our favorite highlights. And every year, Jerry and I made sure we took a trip without the children.

Diana did well in school and was also identified as gifted. She had many friends and was elected class president. After her high school graduation, I thought it was important for her to move out of the house, go to college, and live on campus. She was very much daddy's little girl, and I thought she needed to learn some independence. She needed to be away from home so that she could grow up and mature.

So when we moved out of Sepulveda, Diana had already started college at San Diego State. Then she transferred to the University of California–San Diego. She later received her bachelor's degree from UCLA and went on to Whittier College, where she got a law degree. However, Diana soon realized she was not interested in practicing law.

Diana once told me that she went to law school because she wanted to please me. She wanted to be like me, but she didn't have the temperament or the ambition. She couldn't be me. Jerry wanted her to be a schoolteacher and blamed me when she did not pursue a career in education. I hope he has accepted that

Diana did and does follow her own calling regardless of what we want.

Diana found an excellent life partner in Greg Turk. Greg, who went to UCLA for his undergraduate degree and graduated from Georgetown University's dental school, is low key and a good complement to Diana's high energy. He is smart and ambitious—an all-American male who's into sports. He is an involved father to their three children, Shayna, Andrew, and Talia. He loves his family, especially our darling daughter, Diana. He works hard in maintaining a private dental practice in Woodland Hills and is a good provider, enabling our daughter to be a full-time mom to their three children.

Diana runs the household and all aspects of their lives. She is a promoter. She knows how to get things done. Once all the children where in school, she started a business from home called People Platters. It is a creative business with personalized clay figures on a platter accessorized with charms to tell about one's interests and personalities. Her website, www.peopleplatters.com, is awesome. Look it up! People love her products, and she gets orders from all over the world. I am very proud of her.

With time, Diana and I weathered the stormy twists and turns of our relationship, and we are doing very well. As she matured, we were able to meet as adults. Diana is still daddy's little girl, but now, with her own husband and children, there is definitely room in her life for me. Our mother-daughter conflicts of yesterday are no longer. Now I can respectfully disagree with her and can appreciate and celebrate the person Diana has become. She is an attractive, competent young woman, still spirited, and with a heart of gold, a treasure to all those in her life, especially me. She's fun to be with, always on the go, and lives life with passion. I feel so lucky to be an important part of her life.

Johnny, too, has come into his own as a cherished son, husband, and father. Some important family changes are relevant to discuss here. When our Sepulveda neighborhood changed and students were bused in from other areas of town, big changes occurred in our household, especially for Johnny. One day a boy accosted him in the locker room with a knife. The kid demanded money. When I heard that, I said, "We are getting out of here."

We sold our house in Sepulveda and bought another one on Corie Lane in West Hills. This was in the Las Virgenes School District, so Johnny was supposed to go to Calabasas High School. He was devastated because he was a sophomore at Monroe High School and wanted to graduate with his friends. Furthermore, Johnny loved playing the saxophone in the band at Monroe. Calabasas did not have a band. He was very upset, but I took my usual tough stance: Too bad. We can't stay in Sepulveda. It's too dangerous.

El Camino High School, close by in Woodland Hills, had a band, so this turned out to be a solution. Since El Camino was part of the Los Angeles School District, Johnny used a friend's address, enrolled there, and was able to join the band and make new friends.

JOHNNY'S WEDDING

Johnny has always been the master of compromise and nego-tiation, traits that serve him so well in his legal career now. He received his bachelor's degree from UCLA and his law degree from Loyola Law School. He is senior vice president at Sony Pictures Legal Affairs. He once said to me, "Mother, I have inherited your cognitive abilities, your logical thinking process, which are a big aid in my job as an attorney." I cherish this affirmation.

The yesterdays seem so far away. My little boy is all grown up, so dashing, tall, and handsome. I feel understood. I feel safe around him whenever the stressors of life knock at my door, and he's there with empathy and support. His clear and focused thinking and his sensitivity of heart are a great comfort to me.

Johnny met his wife, Gail Becker, at UCLA when they were students. My son married a woman who is a lot like me: smart and ambitious. In the department of looks, she's an absolute knockout. Best of all, she is a devoted mother and loves my son. I know—a mother knows. When he was little, Johnny used to say he wanted to marry me. I told him I was already spoken for, but someday he would find a little girl just like me. And he did in Gail. They are a high-powered, dual-career couple.

Gail gives him a run for his money. She graduated from Northwestern University with a master's in journalism. She started her career as a news correspondent with the NBC affiliate in Beaumont, Texas, followed by a position as director of communications for the United States Department of Health and Human Services under Donna Shalala in the Clinton Administration. Then, she became vice president of communications for Warner Bros. Home Entertainment, and now she serves as the president of the western region and chairperson of Canada and Latin America for Edelman, the world's largest independent public relations firm.

Gail is the first to acknowledge that without Johnny, she could not do what she does. Like his father before him, he cleans, markets, does laundry, and is very nurturing with their two sons, Joshua and Eli.

I am happy to see that my children are friends with their spouses. They have a connection beyond being parents to their children. That will hold them in good stead when the children are grown and out of the house.

I often wonder what my children really think of me, good and bad. Does a parent ever get to know? Do children ever feel safe enough to tell their parents how they really feel? I hope and trust that my children feel secure enough in my devotion to them to humor me and critique my relationship with them, past and present (see Diana and Johnny's contributions in the Appendix). There is nothing I can do about the past, but today I try to be the best parent I can be.

GRANDCHILDREN

Destiny has granted me five precocious, unique grandchildren, with none their equal (this is their grandmother talking). They call me Bubbe, Yiddish for grandmother. My sister said, "But Bubbe means an old lady. Why would you want to be called an old lady?" I said, "Because I am!" I don't recall observing my own children when they first walked and talked. Now, with my grandchildren, I was and am aware of the joy of watching them evolve through their critical stages of development.

I feel so privileged to experience "grandmotherhood."

I never imagined how special and enriching Bubbe status could be. How could I have known? Many moons ago, pregrandchildren, my friend Bobbie once predicted, "Wait until you have grandchildren." I recall thinking: *How would she, how could she know how I'm going to feel?* I was truly concerned that I might not be able to feel the way she did. After all, having grandchildren was never a goal of mine. Years back, I once said to my son, Johnny, "If I die tomorrow, don't cry over me. I've had a wonderful life and experienced it all."

"But Mother," he exclaimed in indignation, "you have not had grandchildren yet." He was right, so very right.

Here are my grandchildren in their own words.

Eli: "I love to play baseball and I like growing and becoming strong. When I grow up, I want to be a tennis player. I like the ribs I eat at Bubbe's house. I love Bubbe. I love books and the monster book I have that I know how to read. I also love my Curious George book. I love to eat the steak my dad makes. I love to travel. My Bubbe is so kind, and I love how my Bubbe gives me lots of money."

Joshua: "My favorite food is steak, and I'm open to trying new things. I will try anything once. When I grow up, I want to be a soccer player, but in case it does not happen, I want to be a lawyer (as I'm very good in arguing my point). I love to travel the world. I love to read books and play soccer and tennis. My Bubbe is very strong, kind, and outgoing. She never has stage fright and speaks her mind."

Talia: "I love to play softball and all other sports. My favorite thing to do is to play on the all-star teams. I love going shopping and being with my friends. My favorite thing about Bubbe is that she is so strong and never gives up and believes in herself and other people. She's very generous to me in so many ways. I also want to go to UCLA or Texas and play on the softball team there. When I grow up, I want to be on the USA Softball Olympic team, and if that doesn't happen, I want to be a dentist like my dad or a psychologist like my Bubbe."

Andrew: "I'm in high school. I'm a straight-A student who absolutely loves sports. Every day of my life consists of something sports-related. Even though Bubbe is not a sports fanatic, I still have a very special relationship with her. She is never afraid to speak her mind and she gets what she wants! I truly love how my Bubbe shares everything she has from her house (for parties) to her money (for trips). I love Bubbe!!"

Shayna: "I'm going into my senior year of high school at New Community Jewish High School. After my graduation, I hope to go to UCLA or Stanford and eventually become a dermatologist. Every year for the past eight years, I have run a drama camp at my Bubbe and Grandpa Jerry's theater called STARS (Shayna Turk Academy of Rising Stars). I lead around twenty-five kids in singing, dancing, and acting, and ultimately I prepare them for the show. It is my favorite thing to do during the year. My Bubbe has helped me so much with these musicals, and it means so much to me. I am so lucky to have my Bubbe. She supports everything I do and is always there for me. When I need any advice or just someone to talk to, she is the first I look to. Over the years, I have gotten closer with her, and I am so glad, because she is such an amazing person and I look up to her. She means the world to me, and I love her to the moon and back. I love you, Bubbe."

I never miss an opportunity to communicate my philosophy of life to my grandchildren. For example, I urge my granddaughters to not become sexually active until they meet their significant others. I tell Shayna and Talia, "My precious granddaughters, listen to your Bubbe. Wait until you are twenty-plus, mature, and wise to have sex." To my grandsons, Andrew, Joshua, and Eli, I say, "Talk with your fathers about sex. They know best."

I am a lucky woman. I am very thankful for all of my grandchildren and for the feelings of plenty and playfulness they elicit in me. I look forward to our life's journey together.

JERUSALEM, 1981

ATHENS,
GREECE, 1981

LONDON, 1985

HOLLAND, 1986

BARBADOS, 1988

ST. THOMAS, 1988

ON FAMILY OUTINGS

In addition to our frequent family functions, the eleven of us (I call us the "little tribe") are creating our history and building memories by traveling together in America and faraway places on a yearly basis. We have been to Mexico, Jamaica, Hawaii, and all over Europe.

It cannot get any better. I am so tickled to live life, to enjoy its riches and challenges, and to be able to share its fruits with our children and grandchildren.

I'm very aware that I am hopelessly enmeshed with my children. If it were up to me, we would all live in one compound, one dwelling, like my parents and grandparents in Tshernovitz. When I don't see my children at least once a week, I shrivel like a plant not watered. Remembering my mother, I use the rod of guilt sparingly. Am I my mother? Ya, of course I am. I miss my mother. I miss my children. I will miss myself when I'm gone.

HANGING OUT MY SHINGLE: DR. ERICA MILLER, PHD

After completing my PhD in clinical psychology, my first job was at the Forte Foundation, a not-for-profit outpatient clinic in Encino that was run by a master's-level clinician. After completing the 2,000 postgraduate hours required for licensing, I took the state exam in San Francisco and missed passing it by five points.

What a disappointment! Five points short of receiving a license. Five points, twenty-five points, what difference does it make? I failed to pass the test, and I hurt! I felt entrapped by the ambiguous multiple-choice questions. I have a good grasp of the English language, but, for example, the difference between mild and moderate eludes me.

The thought of going through that exam again made me look around at alternatives. A colleague suggested I get the Marriage, Family, and Child Counseling license. That's what I did. After reading and studying in the marriage and family field, I took the written and oral exams and passed with flying colors. I was licensed as a marriage and family therapist, with a PhD in clinical psychology. That was fine with me. I was tired, very tired. I was not about to face the licensing board again, and that was that! The important thing for me was the title Dr. Miller. No one can ever take this title away from me.

At the Forte Foundation, the executive director made me her executive administrative assistant, with an office next to hers. I was on the telephone handling intakes and assigning patients to staff members. I loved the control. I must confess that I took advantage of my position and assigned myself the patients that sounded interesting, divvying out the rest to other counselors. I had the status of the title "doctor" and enjoyed the clinical work and the respect of my colleagues. I was there for several years.

I loved being a clinician. I liked the process of psychological testing and long-term psychotherapy. Understanding a client's background was essential to formulating an individualized action plan to assist and promote wellness. My strategy was assessment first and diagnosis second. Then and only then was it time to cognitively coach the person to overcome the maladaptive past and to problem-solve new ways of living in this world.

At staff meetings, counselors began turning to me for supervisory input where formerly they had sought input from the executive director. Everybody came to me for feedback because the executive director was burdened with paperwork and administrative tasks and had become more and more isolated. She did all of the grunt work and I got the glory. When she saw what was happening, she took action. She took me off the telephone. I was no longer in charge of intakes. In effect, she dried up my referral sources as a first step in getting rid of me. There may have been other reasons as well. I assumed that my presence was too much for her to bear.

I decided it was time for me to move on. One of my placements during training at Forte had been in a Beverly Hills clinic in which neurotic patients were seen individually and in group settings. For several years, while at Forte, I facilitated both women's and men's groups. When I left the Forte Foundation, those patients followed me to my new location.

Looking back, I feel bad about what happened to the executive director after I left and opened my own practice. The patients followed me, and the economic loss must have been devastating for her. Later in my own clinics, the same thing happened to me. What goes around comes around. Did I say that before? Sure I did. Some sayings are worth repeating.

MILLER PSYCHOLOGICAL CENTERS

In 1983 I told Jerry I was leaving the Forte Foundation and opening my own practice. "Don't worry," he said. "I'll get you clients." He began attending union meetings and contacted the presidents of the different chapters, informing them of our services and our willingness to accept their insurance as payment in full. Jerry worked out contracts with Pacific Bell in Northridge, with the Retail Clerks Union in Los Angeles, and with employee assistance programs. After a couple of years, we landed the huge Union 990 contract, representing Los Angeles County employees. Since we agreed to accept insurance as payment in full, the union members could be seen as they needed to be, without paying out of pocket. It was good for employees; it was good for us.

We opened the first Miller Psychological Centers office in Tarzana, California. The three best counselors at the Forte Foundation joined my practice. They had faith that Jerry could generate patients and that under my leadership they would likely grow as clinicians and benefit financially as well.

In ten years, Miller Psychological Centers grew from three

therapists to forty multidisciplinary clinicians, including marriage and family counselors, social workers, clinical psychologists, and psychiatrists.

True to his word, Jerry worked with unions and streamlined the referral of patients to our clinic. I, on the other hand, attended meetings at the union hall on a regular basis, free of charge, to help mediate conflicts between middle management and shop stewards. There was constant pulling and pushing between union leaders and management. I had an aptitude for conflict resolution. I became a mediator as well as an intervention trainer. I taught the shop stewards and supervisors how to identify troubled workers and intervene with counseling before situations got out of hand and put their jobs at risk. Jerry opened the doors to the union clientele, and I showed them firsthand what counseling could do.

The unions sent us all of their employees who needed counseling. They alluded to us that if we were to open offices closer to where their employees lived, they could refer many more clients. Within a year after we opened Miller Psychological Centers in Tarzana, we added eight more offices all over Los Angeles and Orange County.

Jerry was instrumental in locating office spaces in strategic places. I hired the clinicians. They were handpicked, skilled therapists, and our excellent reputation brought a steady stream of new referrals. The phone was ringing off the hook. Those were exciting days!

Miller Psychological Centers was providing high-quality psychological services to hundreds of workers and had become a thriving, successful business. Jerry was the rainmaker and I was the administrative CEO.

I did not start out with the goal of opening multiple offices. Like any first-class novice entrepreneur, I was ready to go with the flow to wherever the opportunity might take me. The business evolved. The demand was there, and we were able to fill it.

Initially I took it upon myself to interview every new patient that came through our doors. I assigned the patient to the clinician who I thought would be best for that person. By arranging a good patient-therapist match and insisting on a battery of testing, I laid the groundwork for getting the best possible help for our patients in the shortest time possible.

Soon I ran out of time to see patients myself. Someone had to do the administrative work of running all of the clinics. I found that I could do it really well. I could have managed twenty clinics. The number didn't matter. It was the format, the system of organization, and strong management that mattered.

My clinical team and I were trained to treat people with their "garden-variety" mental health issues, not alcohol or drug addictions. The huge need for treatment of substance abuse soon became apparent. That was not what we did. I had no training in alcohol- and drug-abuse treatment. I decided we should hire an expert in the field. Again, Jerry was instrumental in locating the right counselor for the job. He went to Alcoholics Anonymous meetings and other substance-abuse recovery programs, scouting for the right person for us.

Jerry met Harry Miyaji in 1988. Harry was working in the field of substance-abuse treatment at an agency in Los Angeles. Jerry was impressed. Harry had been in the trenches, having battled a substance-abuse problem himself, and had been in recovery for many years.

When I met Harry, it was clear to me that he would be an asset. I liked him, and there was an instant connection. I appointed him as a supervisor in charge of our drug and alcohol department. He had the expertise and we had the clients. We now had two corporations: Miller Psychological Centers and California Diversion Intervention Foundation (CDIF). We incorporated CDIF separately, as a nonprofit organization.

MY PHILOSOPHY AS A THERAPIST

Therapy. What is therapy? According to the dictionary, "therapy is a procedure designed to treat disease, illness, or disability." In other words, therapy is a process, a series of steps toward a desired outcome marked by gradual, intrinsic change that is rarely visible to the naked eye.

Achieving the desired outcome definitely depends on a positive relationship between the client and the clinician. The readiness of the patient and the skills of the therapist also are key, as are the therapist's intuition, empathy, and a strong conveyed belief that change is possible. It does not matter what theory of change the therapist utilizes—Freudian or Rogerian, psychodynamic or behaviorist.

My therapy style is eclectic—a little bit of this, a little bit of that. I view myself as an instructor, coach, mentor, and preacher. I try to convey to my clients that life is to be lived today. The past is gone, and the future might never be. I am committed to inspire and influence them to join me in the here and now as I impart my knowledge, spirit, passion, and appreciation for life with all of its twists and turns.

My orientation is psychodynamic—a moving, evolving process of uncovering layers of the past and learning new perspectives and behaviors. A person experiencing a toothache or a physical pain rushes to see a doctor. The same is not true regarding psychological discomfort. Some people drag around pounds upon pounds of old baggage before ending up at the doorsteps of a mental health professional.

It is amazing to me that in spite of the many pop psychologist talk shows on radio and TV and the massive body of information at hand, the stigma of going to therapy persists.

What happened to the voices of reason? A healthy mind and body are essential for the well-being of the whole person! Hey, voices of reason, speak louder! We, the people, need to hear you!

In the initial session, after introducing myself and my qualifications, I affirm the new patient for being in my office. I proceed to tell them the aforementioned—how society still views a heartache as different from a heart attack. The irony is that frequently, stress, anger, anxiety, and heartache are precursors to heart attacks.

I further inform them that before I can alleviate their psychic pain and help them problem-solve, I must ask them many questions: "Why are you here? Why now? What do you hope to achieve?"

In a medical diagnosis, a doctor does not prescribe medication before carrying out fact-finding procedures. The same holds true in a psychological evaluation. With their permission, I will get to know them, get to know what makes them tick, before I make any recommendation.

They have been struggling for a long time on their own. Now there are two of us. Two heads are better than one—and it's always us, us, us. My goal is to facilitate a strong bond between us to help them feel safe, to assure them they are not alone. In me they have a partner to see them through the search for themselves.

The diagnostic process, which includes psychological testing, lasts for three sessions. In our fourth session I share with them their test results and give them my clinical impressions. Often they are amazed at my assessment. They feel heard and understood, perhaps for the first time in their lives.

I tell them they can leave at that point if they choose to, since they have an understanding of what ails them and perhaps that is all they want at that moment. On the other hand, if they want to work on any of the issues of concern we've identified, I suggest a commitment of at least three to six months.

I tell them that they have the pain, and I have the training and clinical knowledge. Together we make a good pair. Change takes time, takes practice, and yet it is definitely possible.

It is clear to me that psychological testing provides a great aid to get to know patients within an accelerated time frame. Testing provides objective data to supplement my impressions from initial interviews.

TAT cards, for example, are a series of pictures of people in various poses that suggest typical life circumstances. The patient tells what he or she sees in the picture and thereby projects his or her own issues into the story. The cards elicit experiences the patient may have had but didn't think to mention. Sometimes nothing comes forward, which is also diagnostically valuable.

A case in point: "Anna," a female patient, was arrested, and she was referred to me by the courts. Counseling was ordered because as a camp counselor she had become sexually involved with a thirteen-year-old boy.

She had been abandoned as an infant at the doorstep of a stranger. She did not know who her parents were. Social services transferred her from one foster home to another. She never fit in;

she never belonged. Now, in her early thirties, she was still acting out early trauma.

When I showed her the TAT card of a man and woman embracing, nothing came forth. She couldn't even formulate what affection meant. Through therapy she came to understand that she was attracted to young boys because she was a young girl emotionally. It was interesting that, from her description, the thirteen-year-old boy she slept with appeared to be quite mature.

The age difference didn't even register consciously. Emotionally, they were peers. Adults barely figured in her world except as cruel authority figures. Such lack of dignity, caring, or warmth in her life had seriously crippled her emotionally.

I doubt that she ever would have been able to form a close relationship with an adult, but I will never know. Eight months into our relationship, she was diagnosed with progressive lung cancer. I visited her frequently in hospice, held her hand, and sat by her bed silently. There was no one in the world for her. She was all alone in life. I am glad I was by her side at the end of her life. I cared for her. I hope she knew it.

Patients often have only screen memories—fleeting vague impressions of enduring disrespect. I was particularly alert to women with relationship issues who settled for abusive partners —women in abusive situations who'd had early faulty attachments that had resulted in withdrawal, poor communication, and an apparent lack of need for people. I advocated a corrective perspective. No, it's not OK to permit that kind of treatment; yes, it's possible to find a loving partner you can trust. The challenge was to teach them self-respect, empowerment, negotiation, compromise, boundaries, and adult ways of resolving conflict.

Many of our court-referred clients were victims of domestic violence. Their stories of cruelty, abuse, and torment were painful reminders of the degradation of human beings that I witnessed as a child. With such clients, I was on a mission to "right" the "wrong" they suffered, for them and for me. I was committed to empower them and assist them to get out of their abusive relationships. To change their system of beliefs, to convince them that they were entitled to a caring and mutually rewarding relationship, was a challenge. A big challenge.

Raising consciousness and promoting change is a painfully long process. I found myself often, way too often, in a race for time.

The theme and the thrust of my work with people focus on understanding where their behaviors and attitudes come from. Then I align with them and pursue the process with little steps until they begin to experience an adult who cares about them and leads them on the path of change. The issue of trust is ever-present in the therapeutic milieu. I encourage them to trust me, as I have no hidden agenda. I have no wants for them. I want to lead them to where they want to go. Whether they do or don't change their lot in life is up to them. My life is not going to change. I am there for them, and I earn their trust over time.

The process of change is exciting and rewarding for the most part. I never recall not liking a patient. What I do recall is the frustration with some patients who were not able or willing to walk all the way to recovery. Wanting a quick fix, unrealistic expectations, and financial constraints are frequent causes of premature termination of therapy.

WORKING WITH CHALLENGING PATIENTS

One patient—I will call him Pete—was referred by the court after a battery charge. During his first visit, he took off his shirt and showed me knife cuts he had inflicted on himself. When he was little, that's what his drunken parents did to him. At age fourteen, Pete ran away from home, from his parents' physical and emotional torture. When he missed them, when he needed to feel alive, he inflicted pain by cutting himself with a knife.

For a patient such as this, one who injures himself, the self-abuse represents "love." He has linked being noticed, being loved, being alive, with pain and punishment. Being hurt put him in touch with his family of origin. He was connected to them through the daily pain and punishment that had become part of his identity. His body was covered with deep wounds. He acted out destructively in other ways as well.

In our weekly sessions, he would use foul language and make comments designed to scare me so that I would reject him. Underneath all of that threatening behavior was a person crying out for help. Assisting Pete, the adult, to nurture and heal the child within would have been a long and painful process. Without a steadfast, long therapeutic relationship (three to five years), Pete's chance of healing the wounds of long ago and experiencing caring relationships with himself and others was nil, zero, nada.

Unfortunately for Pete, after seeing me twice a week for several months in which he tried all kinds of strategies to elicit rejection from me, he attacked someone and ended up in jail. It turned out that he'd intended to get caught. The therapeutic relationship was too much for him. My steadfast, attentive listening and continuous affirmation of his plight were more than he could bear. He was not ready for the therapeutic journey.

Years later, I received a phone call from San Bernardino County. It was Pete. He said, "All that time I was in jail, your presence was with me. I could hear your voice and remember the effect our talks in your office had on me. I could not tolerate your kind presence in your office, but I welcomed it in the isolation of my cell. I'm out of jail now, and I would like to stop harming myself and others. I have a job with a plumbing company in the city of Orange, and it's too far for me to come to your office in Tarzana.

Could you recommend a therapist where I live?" It was gratifying to hear that he was seeking help. I hope he turned his life around.

In the presence of violent patients, it was important that I presented a calm demeanor. I verbalized emphatically that I was not afraid of them. I didn't buy their "bad-boy syndrome" (or "bad-girl syndrome") way of getting attention, nor did I judge them. I took the position, "Let's find out where this maladaptive pattern comes from and decide what you want to do about it." I set boundaries and established parameters: "You can yell. You can emote, but you can't touch me. You break this rule and you're history." At times colleagues, hearing a big ruckus in my office, knocked on my door to make sure I was safe.

"I respect your right to kill yourself if you must," I would tell suicidal patients. "The only thing I ask of you is that, before you kill yourself, you call me first. Maybe I can talk you out of it; maybe not. Life is going to go on with or without you. I care what happens to you; however, I'm not willing to invest in our relationship unless you are. If you cannot commit to us, I will refer you to another therapist in a heartbeat! So what will it be?" As luck has it, I never lost a patient due to suicide.

Patients who experience repeated trauma, especially early in life, benefit from a strong therapeutic bond, often built up over several years. The longest I ever saw a patient was about five years.

Once, I was privileged to attend a supervisory session for psychologists, led by a famous analyst. Several seasoned clinicians were invited to present cases of their most challenging patients for her clinical observations. I presented a young man whom I used to call "my pet." My question to the analyst was, "How long is long enough?

At that point, after I had been treating him for four years, I wondered, "Am I keeping him in therapy for me or for him?" He was unable to choose to leave me, so it was my responsibility to send him on his way when I thought he was ready. "Well, when will that be?" I asked. She assured me that six or seven years of therapy is not unusual with this kind of case history.

My "pet" (I will call him Mark) came from an Orthodox Jewish family from Poland. When he was a few months old, his mother developed tuberculosis and was in and out of hospitals. Other relatives cared for him, passing him around from family to family, and he never had an opportunity to bond with one significant person. Consequently, he suffered from early attachment deficit. His wife, "Ann," who was divorcing him, was worried about his mental stability and literally dragged him to my office. She was right. He was a basket case.

As a teenager, Mark got Ann, then his sixteen-year-old Christian girlfriend, pregnant. He did the "right thing" and married her—to the dismay of his family, who cut him out of their lives. The young couple made a home in Los Angeles and raised a family. Over the years, the relationship deteriorated. His wife couldn't reach him emotionally. When Ann asked him for a divorce, he was devastated. Here he had done the right thing by marrying the mother of his child, losing his family of origin in the process, and now his wife was abandoning him as well.

He was one of the most depressed people I have ever seen. Fortunately, he had the financial resources to make good use of therapy. I saw him three times a week over many years. My accent, similar to that of his family of origin, was an asset in our relationship.

Treatment was a long and painful process. I talked to everyone about him. I got the best supervision I could find. I became very attached to him. I confessed to my colleagues not once but many times that I wished I could take him home and make him "whole." Treatment centered on building trust and transferring the nurturing he felt from me to himself. He reluctantly shared a recurring dream in which I hovered over him like a spirit from above, engulfing him with soothing repetitive words, "You are OK. You will be OK. Sleep, my child, sleep." The healing process was under way.

Eventually, I pushed him gently out of the nest. Mark moved back to Connecticut, where he was originally from, and made peace with his family—one of the rewarding fruits of therapy for me. That was a very positive step for him and provided a bridge from terminating with me to moving forward with his life. I was proud of our accomplishment. I thought it was a meaningful, orchestrated finale to our relationship. Or was it?

I confess that my countertransference—emotional entanglement with a patient—was at play when I allowed him to continue seeing me in therapy for quite a while, even when he began having financial difficulties, without insisting that he pay me regularly, cut back on his sessions, or both.

When Mark left treatment, he owed me ten thousand dollars. He promised he would pay me every penny if it were the last thing he did. I believed him based on his history of always paying on time. He would come into my office, and before he would sit down on my couch, he would hand me his check, like clockwork.

When his reversal of monetary fortune should have prevented him from continuing treatment, I assured him it was all right to continue his therapy and he could pay me back as soon as he was able. He never came through.

Well, if I experienced countertransference toward him, why would I think that transference was not in play when he decided it was OK to owe or not pay back to one's "family," especially if the family rejected him? I asked myself, "Was I his family? Did he need to punish me?"

Never before or since have I allowed a patient to owe me money. I messed up. Dual relationships have no place in a therapeutic setting.

It's rare that I hear from a patient once therapy has terminated. Well, I ran into Mark many years later. I was at a social gathering and there he was, just standing there. I looked at him and he looked at me. We were both amazed and excited to see each other.

He said to me, "I don't know how you did it. It was not like I had a sudden revelation and I was 'therapized.' I do not know or care how you did it. What I do know is, thanks to you, I'm a different man now and I feel good about my life. I am remarried, we have a child together, I'm doing well in business—a far cry from the depressed, lost soul I was when you first met me."

His new wife approached, and he introduced us. "I am someone from your husband's past," I said.

"Wait a minute," she exclaimed, "are you a therapist?"

"He was one of my former students," I answered.

"He talks about you often," she said.

"Well," I said, "I readied him for you."

After talking a few more minutes, I quickly found Jerry and left. It was important to me not to socialize with patients, whether former or current. But I certainly was delighted to find out he was doing so well—that I had, in fact, made a difference. I never brought up his debt. Neither did he. It remains unfinished business for both of us. Letting go is a hard thing to do!

Another patient of mine comes to mind. The issue was his bisexuality. It was a problem for his wife, not for him. "If it feels good, no matter what gender, what's the big deal," he would say. To the dismay of his wife, I could not be of help. He liked being bisexual. The marriage ended in divorce. This patient was very provocative. He wanted to meet me outside the office and start a friendship once we terminated therapy. I explained to him the rules against dual relationships. Once I become a friend, I could never be an objective therapist should he need to see me in the future.

I never fraternized with clients. The temptation is there. You spend hours with a person over the course of years. You "fix" them. But when they are all "perfect," you say good-bye, never to see them again. It's all about professional boundaries.

I do not condone, but I do understand, those therapists who rationalize and develop personal relationships with ex-patients. I attest to the fact that I never acted on my countertransference feelings. My rich fantasy life is mine to experience and not to act on. Thanks to the stars above, I know the difference.

I always wondered how I would react if a patient walked into my office speaking in a German accent. What if he or she reminded me of the Nazis?

One of my supervisors, Dr. Sharma, a very wise psychiatrist, said once that we as individuals are not suited to treat everyone. We need to know when to refer a case. I couldn't imagine someone I couldn't relate to—from the severely mentally ill to the court-referred offenders—except for a Nazi.

One day, a new patient with a thick German accent called for an appointment. She was a referral from a previous client. I heard the German accent over the phone and pondered. I decided to observe myself, to see what my reaction would be, once I was in the presence of someone who was, to me, a potential Nazi.

Somewhat apprehensive, I opened the door to greet "Rosa," a short and zaftig (chubby) woman with dark hair and brown eyes. Not very Arian. Her dilemma was that her sixteen-year-old daughter was acting out, would not respect her parents' rules, and caused great turmoil in the household. The father, a very strict parent, would hardly let the daughter out of the house, so she would go out the window. He refused to come to counseling. Rosa was highly stressed because her life with her husband and daughter was out of control.

Perhaps, who knows, her own father had been a member of the Gestapo, but that never came into play. I never asked when they came to this country or who her parents were. It didn't matter. I did not care. I was able to relate to her just as to any other client in pain. My European background was an advantage. I was able to persuade her husband, "Leo," a businessman, to come in and consult with me. I made sure to mention that I needed his input, not to help him but to straighten out his daughter, who caused grief to his wife.

In my office, I listened carefully to his complaints and aligned with him by commenting on Americans' less strict style of parenting. I also said, "You might be right about your daughter. She lives in your house and has to abide by your rules. It is not all right for her to sneak out and disobey you! But she does. What is a parent to do? Let's put our heads together and see what can be done. Two heads are better than one. No disrespect to your head!" He gave me an unexpected grin. I did some short-term intervention, and it worked. He was able to lighten up somewhat on his demands. His daughter agreed to adhere to modified rules, and the family was able to coexist.

My concrete approach and problem-solving strategies worked well with Leo, as it did with other corporate or business-type men who were initially resistant. The win-win concept that works well in business also works in personal relationships.

A NEW TREATMENT—AND A SCARY MOMENT

After working with psychotherapy clients for several years, I decided to add another technique to my knowledge base (aka bag of tricks). I took a course in hypnotherapy. I wanted to learn how to use clinical hypnosis. I had several long-term patients whose problems were deeply entrenched, and it was hard to get through to their core issues.

Clinical studies show that sometimes, with repressed patients, hypnosis can relax defenses and access early childhood trauma that is interfering in their adult functioning. I hoped that this technique would come in handy when I encountered deep, locked doors of their vulnerable psyche.

The University of California–Santa Barbara, offered a hypnotherapy course once a week for six months, culminating in the certification to engage in hypnotherapy. The instructor, Dr. Goodman, used role-playing, practice with one another, and materials from real case studies. When we mastered basic techniques, we were asked to practice on our own clients, those whom we deemed appropriate for this kind of treatment.

The criterion for choosing our first client to practice on was their consent. At the university when we practiced on each other, I was skeptical and unwilling or unable to relax enough to be a good subject for an altered state. Even though I learned that the hypnotist does not have the power to compel or coerce a person who agrees to be hypnotized—because no one does anything he or she doesn't want to (even while in a trance)—I knew it wouldn't work for me because of my issues with control.

More than once when Jerry and I had parties, we hired a hypnotist and witnessed in amazement how quickly Jerry, Diana, and some of our guests could "go under." They were suggestible and able to let go. They were good subjects. I, on the other hand, could close my eyes until doomsday, but there was no way I was going to go under.

After a few months of training, I decided it was time to try out my new skills. The first patient on whom I practiced hypnotherapy was "Julio," a thirty-eight-year-old man whom I had seen for several years. He had huge memory blocks.

He was from South America, and his wife was born in the U.S. They had entrenched marital issues around his need to be number one and keep his wife second in command, as his culture dictated, but which she found objectionable. They were both educated and knew better, but he had such a struggle with early conditioning, including early abandonment and other traumas, none of which he could remember.

One day I asked his permission to try something different. He agreed to allow the experience of an altered state. I explained that, afterward, he could share only what he wished about his images and experiences. I proceeded to count to ten, and then I suggested walking through a meadow, feeling very peaceful and so forth. I suggested that he go back to when he was a little boy and asked him how old he was and what was happening.

He said almost nothing but whimpered in a childish voice, exhibiting frightening expressions, moving his head left and right with his body limp, except for a few convulsive tremors. Suddenly, he stopped any kind of movement and appeared almost comatose. I inquired about his state of mind: "Hey Julio, where are you? What do you see?"

He didn't respond to my questions like Dr. Goodman had said he would. He just lay there. I started being concerned. I wondered what I should do next. "A while ago, I saw you being agitated, frightened—what happened?" I asked. He was supposed to respond to my questions, so why didn't he? *I am doing something wrong,* I thought. *OK, I might as well bring this to a conclusion. It didn't work.*

I said, "Now it's time to come back from being a child, back to the present time, here in 1983 in Los Angeles. I will count to ten, and when I say ten, you will open your eyes and be back in your normal, adult self, feeling relaxed, refreshed, and comfortable." When I got to the count of ten again, nothing happened. He just lay there. No movement, nothing—absolutely still, like a corpse.

I began to feel a hint of panic—not much, just a hint. I swallowed hard and said, "OK, Julio, our time is nearly up. It's time to come back to the present moment." My tone of voice changed from soothing to assertive. "I'm going to start counting again, and when I reach ten and I clap my hands, you are going to be awake, refreshed." When I reached the number ten, the same thing happened. He didn't move a muscle.

Now I was really scared. *What do I do next?* In a firm, low voice I said, "Well, you will lie there as long as you need to. I'm leaving the room now. My next patient is due in a few minutes. If you are still here when I return, I shall see my next patient in another consulting room, and you will leave as soon as you are ready to. I'm leaving now!"

When I stood up as if to leave, he opened his eyes and sat up on the couch in a daze. "Julio," I exclaimed, "I am glad you are up. Now I don't need to use another room for my next patient. We will talk about your experience next session."

"I was so comfortable and relaxed," he said. "I heard your voice, but I didn't want to come back. I just wanted to stay in that peaceful place forever."

"That's OK. Let's talk about it next time. I need to go now," I told him.

Back in class, I expressed my dismay to my instructor: "Dr. Goodman, you didn't tell me that this could happen!" The other students listened as I related my experience. He said, "That's a good lesson for all of you. You will never lose a patient. He or she will always come out of the trance." That was reassuring news. I wish I'd had the information when I needed it.

In Julio's case, we actually did get to some repressed material that was helpful in his treatment.

Our instructor told us that hypnosis doesn't work with eating disorders, among other things, and has a poor success rate with smoking cessation. I did not believe him. *Don't tell me it cannot be done!* I tried hypnotherapy with overeaters, and he was right. It did not work.

A CASUALTY OF HMOS

The early 1990s was the beginning of the end of our garden-variety clientele. The health maintenance organizations (HMOs) were forming. We told our patients to be sure to sign up and continue with their Blue Cross coverage. Otherwise they wouldn't be able to continue seeing their therapists at Miller. At insurance enrollment time, employees were given an option to choose either the new Kaiser HMO, which had its own therapists, or continue with Blue Cross as in the past.

The HMOs made the package so attractive that almost everyone signed up for this cheaper option. The union members all left Blue Cross and went to Kaiser for their insurance. The benefits, in general, were so much better. Only those with expensive private insurance could continue at Miller. Such clients were few and far between.

The boom we had enjoyed since 1984 went bust. In 1994, Miller Psychological Centers went under. I was occupying twelve lovely remodeled suites in our main office in Tarzana when the bottom fell out. I had a five-year lease. At our other locations I had month-to-month leases, so I wasn't as concerned about those.

I went into problem-solving mode. I tried to hold on to the Tarzana office, which we were renting for five thousand dollars a month, by subletting some of the rooms to therapists at large. I tried to hold on for dear life. I told the landlord that I would give him two thousand dollars a month for four of our offices, plus all of the proceeds from renting the other eight beautiful suites, but he said no. We had to vacate the premises, and Miller Psychological Centers sadly declared bankruptcy.

CDIF CONTINUES

My defense mechanisms of detachment came to my rescue once more. It is what it is. Life is unpredictable. Ups and downs, twists and turns of our destiny just happen. I did nothing wrong. I could not fight HMOs—so what? Move on! What to do? We were down, but not completely out.

Jerry thought I should quit and fold my tent. It was too difficult to compete with the HMOs, the Walmart of mental health). I said, "No way! I'm not about to cave in to the pressure of the changing tide of private mental health services." We still had the nonprofit company, CDIF.

Over the years, under the leadership of Harry, our drug and alcohol department supervisor, we developed good contacts with the courts and probation departments of Los Angeles and Orange County. Being on the referral list meant we could provide services for their court-referred clients who needed treatment and rehabilitation for substance abuse, domestic violence, and anger management in lieu of incarceration.

In all of our office locations where we had month-to-month leases, we downsized and retained one group room so that Harry could continue to run the diversion programs. We were battered but not defeated! I was still in business. The tide was rising once more. We were hanging in there! There was hope. *Don't tell me it cannot be done!*

I promoted Harry to program director, and I remained the

administrative CEO. It worked well for both of us. We built on what we had left, and we continued building.

Presently, we provide outpatient mental health services in ten locations all over Los Angeles and Orange County (Granada Hills, West Los Angeles, Whittier, Hawthorne, Montebello, Norwalk, City of Orange, Garden Grove, Anaheim, and Catalina). Most, if not all, of our drug-certified counselors have been through recovery, spent time in jail, and know the ropes. They are able to guide and inspire our clients like no other. They have been down and out and made it after all. They are good role models.

The six- to twelve-month-long court-prescribed programs we offer are intended to rehabilitate and keep offenders from the revolving doors of the penal system. The message the courts convey is loud and clear: "Turn your life around or you go to jail. You are given an opportunity through education, counseling, and support to stop abusing and/or selling drugs, to stop engaging in domestic violence and petty theft, and to overcome your sexual addictions. All these destructive behaviors affect you, your family, and society at large. We won't have it. It is against the law!"

The court-appointed monitoring agencies "honor" us with frequent, unexpected visits. They sit in on ongoing group sessions, observe the counselors and group dynamic, and check client files for timely progress reports. I like it. It keeps us on the straight and narrow. Very rarely, following these unannounced visits, are we written up for an infraction. All in all, we are doing well. We continue being recertified year in and year out by the state of California and remain on the much coveted referral list.

Some outpatient mental health agencies like ours have been closed due to irregularities. I keep tight control, overseeing and supervising our operation so that doesn't happen to us. We have had to dismiss counselors for various reasons, including when they have fallen off the wagon (and started using drugs or alcohol again), have become sexually involved with clients, or have pocketed money received they received from clients.

When that happens, when a counselor falls by the wayside, we act quickly before they can do further damage. We are good employers, offering medical benefits to our full-time counselors and allowances for gas and car upkeep.

My MO is, "If you do not treat your employees right and compensate them well, they will leave you, and they should. This is America, the land of the free, the land of opportunity." So far, in thirty years of being an employer, no one ever left because of poor working conditions or less pay than their counterparts at other agencies.

A revolving door of employees is detrimental to any business, yet I will never be held hostage by anyone. My mantra: "If you are unhappy, if you do not think you are getting paid enough, then find another job. You owe it to yourself. I will give you a going-away party." Most of our counselors seem to be doing well at work, in their personal relationships, and in their economic endeavors.

It is worth mentioning that in addition to CDIF in 1998, I partnered with Harry Miyaji and founded a for-profit corporation called California Long-Term Care (CLTC). The thought behind this enterprise was to inspire and enable our counselors to venture into startup businesses such as car detailing, janitorial services, or any other business they might have been interested in. I would remind them in our staff meetings that under the umbrella of CLTC, with an 800 number, accounting, and legal services already in place, they could have an opportunity to own a portion of a business. We would provide initial capital investment, and we would work out the details of the limited partnership.

I thought it was a great opportunity for some or all of our employees to experience and participate in a capitalistic venture, in an American dream. So far, no one has taken us up on our offer. It is hard for most people to take the leap into entrepreneurial ventures.

I remain open to new ventures that may come my way so that I stay challenged until I fade away at the ripe old age of 100-plus. In the meantime, as always, I spend my energy on my challenges at hand, in the here and now, in all aspects of my life—as a CEO, wife, mother, grandmother, author, and lecturer. The here and now looks good, very good!

I still enjoy counseling, especially imparting effective parenting skills to couples, as well as working with adults on their short-term issues. My schedule has become too busy for me to work with the severely troubled long-term patients. Between my administrative and supervisory obligations at my clinics, my extensive travel, and increased lecture engagements, I simply have run out of time. One lifetime is not sufficient to do it all.

THE PRESENT

It has been more than six years since our house burned to the ground. Looking at it today, you would not know it. It looks spectacular. Our rustic, beautiful, fifty-year-old dwelling had a face and body transformation and looks today like a two-year-old house. We definitely were fortunate to turn the lemon of our traumatic event to the sweetest lemonade ever. Are we lucky or what?

My dear readers, I am unabashedly compelled to share with you my appreciation for the gift of my life that keeps on giving, time and again.

Please forgive me for repeating myself so often throughout the pages of my memoir. Here I am, a seventy-eight-year-old young senior in the prime of my life. I can't and won't be bothered by my advanced chronological age and its deemed or prescribed limitations. It is not over until the fat lady sings. To me, my age is irrelevant. I will never succumb to the pressure of society dictating when, how, and what I should be doing at any stage of my life.

I have no desire or intent to slow down. Why would I? I have the drive and energy to continue my many ventures and to remain open to new ones to come.

I hope and trust that I have many more beats left in my battery of life, to keep on going way into the future.

In addition to overseeing the operation of my ten mental health clinics, I have recently taken over managing our properties in Austin, Texas. We are now a proud "owner-operated" management company, which has brought welcome challenges to my already rich life.

I'm proud to mention that I frequently lecture to senior audiences on the subject closest to my heart: psychological aspects of aging. My message is loud and clear: Senior limitations are frequently self-imposed. We seniors are the fastest-growing segment of our population. Many of us do well into our nineties and beyond. "What are you going to do with the rest of your life?" is my ongoing mantra.

I inform, instruct, and inspire. Genetics, although important, are but a portion to contend with. Our healthy lifestyles, strong support system, and positive attitudes are essential ingredients to personal wellness and long life.

My lectures always end with my daughter's flattering remarks, "Mother, I can't keep up with you! If we could bottle your energy, spirit, and optimism, we could make a fortune." Wouldn't you like to hear similar comments from your daughter? Go get them! Tomorrow is the first day of the rest of your life.

A PREDICTION

I have been there, done that. I lived three lives and died at the ripe old age of 104.

On November 10, 2037, I expired peacefully in my sleep, as I so often envisioned, becoming one with the universe. It was my 104th birthday. My children, Diana and Johnny—my pride and joy—and their mates, children, and grandchildren were all there saying their good-byes somberly. They smiled, they cried, they hugged and remembered.

OUR FAMILY, 2009

REFLECTIONS

ON BEING WHO I AM

When people ask me where I'm from and I say Rumania, I can't even think of it as my country. My memory of Rumania comprises filth, poverty, and oppression. I didn't have a chance to put down roots and feel bonded to my birthplace. When I'm asked, "What's your origin?" Rumanian really doesn't fit me.

When Jerry and I traveled to Bucharest, the capital of Rumania, several years ago to revisit some of the places of my childhood, there was no familiarity or feelings of kinship. I felt completely detached. It was just a city in which I had once lived.

I was almost sixteen when we immigrated to Israel. There, although I felt safe and free, I was a new immigrant, and I was mocked by the natives for talking funny. I grew to love Israel, but it was not my origin or my birthplace.

So, where am I from?

When I came to the United States, my manner often shocked Americans. I was too direct, too brazen, too outspoken, and I said what was on my mind, as I had in Israel. One evening, my mother-in-law, a hefty, buxom woman and a widow, was excitedly preparing to meet a blind date. She paraded around in a tight, red knit dress—which, she informed me, was brand new.

She looked like a cheap overstuffed doll. She asked me how I liked it. As politely as I could, I said, "Well, red is a very strong color." I tried to be diplomatic. "You don't know the man; he might be conservative." She became very upset. "All my friends," she huffed, "think I look very good in this dress. Only you don't like it," and off she went.

I think that was the first and last time I ever gave her my opinion. Being direct rather than popular was what I loved about the Israelis. It became my way. There is nothing phony about me. What you see is what you get. I like that about me. If being a straight shooter gets me in trouble once in a while, so be it.

Case in point: When our children were small, I embarrassed them numerous times in front of their friends. When we lived in Sepulveda, Johnny had a little friend, Mikey. I heard that Mikey was always making derogatory remarks about Jews. I didn't like it. One day as we got into our car, he came up to us and asked, "Where are you going?" Johnny told him we were on our way to Disneyland. "Oh," he exclaimed. "You're going to Jew-land."

I let him have it. "Mikey," I shouted, "I don't ever want to hear such remarks out of you. If you can't stop your Jew remarks you will never be allowed in our home again. Do you hear me?" I can still see his sheepish little face, bewildered at my tirade.

Later, Jerry and the kids jumped on me. They thought that I had overreacted. Johnny said, "It is not a big deal, Mom."

"He is just a kid and did not mean anything by it," Jerry echoed.

I did not think so. It was a big deal for me. Whenever I was the target of anti-Semitic comments, I always spoke up. I took a stand. I got involved. I'm sorry that neither of my kids followed in my footsteps on that point. They don't like my trait of being up-front. They might respect the heck out of me. I know they do, but they think I'm too outspoken. Am I?

Once I attended a lecture given by Elie Wiesel, the author and concentration camp survivor. His memorable and poignant views on humanity and the lack thereof are too many to mention. What stand out in my mind are his comments on apathy: "Apathy is the worst of human traits; not getting involved, looking the other way, witnessing brutality from man to man, and not speaking out is unconscionable." We are our brothers' keepers!

I am proud to attest that apathy is not part of my being.

Growing up in Israel, I used to hear that Americans were phony. Well, often they are. Americans embrace that singsong-y, overdone "Hi! How are you?"—without really listening to the answer. Americans think they have to be nice and polite all the time—but I think it's not natural; it makes you two-faced. My mother-in-law, for example, would greet me with, "Oh, hi honey, how are you?" I would respond honestly: "I just had a tooth pulled and

I hurt." She would continue her agenda without missing a beat: "Oh, how wonderful. I went shopping yesterday, and . . ."

To this day, when someone asks, "How are you?" I say, "In which department of my life? What do you want to know?" When my little granddaughter, six years old at the time, pointed downward and said, "It hurts here," I said, "Where is here?"

"My pee-pee," she said.

"That is called a vagina," I corrected her. She became obsessed with this new word. She went around saying, "This is my vagina. This is my private part, my vagina," to the consternation of her dad, my son-in-law, Greg, who exclaimed, "Enough already about the vagina!" Then she moved on to "fart," "booger," and other "bad" words!

Many people have told me at various times, "You are refreshing—you say aloud what other people dare not utter." I cherish those comments. I am an individualist who believes that in order to have a healthy society, we have to strive for healthy, self-actualized people. I consider myself to be such a person. As such, I have the right and obligation to express myself in order to explore uncharted territories, to follow my path even if it means not conforming to the social norms and expectations of others, and to live life according to Erica.

I have climbed my mountains. I'm over the rainbow, living the dream of a life. I am a wife, mother, and grandmother and have the most rewarding professional life. I have it all. I'm very devoted to all of these roles. I strive to be the very best I can be. I do not take my relationships for granted. I do not seek conflict, but I also do not avoid it, often to the consternation of my family.

When my feelings are hurt, I make sure I express them and talk things through. I think it is important to air one's feelings and to be heard. Everyone matters, but so do I. Making a case for my position and listening to theirs affirms the relationship and the individual as well.

I may not be an actress, but I have been on the stage of life, orchestrating people and events to keep on proving time and again that I am the little engine that could. My mantra was, is, and always will be, "Don't tell me I cannot do it," whether because I am a woman, a Jew, a wife, a mother, a grandmother, plain, gorgeous, short, or tall.

I flexed my muscles of ability to receive my PhD while married with two children. How else can I have people look up to me? After all, I stand only five feet tall.

I might not be Dr. Laura, I might not have name recognition yet, but I am going to be published. My story will be on the screen! I know it! I envision it! If not, so be it, but not because I have not tried.

My life has been and continues to be a wonderful journey as I proceed through the stages of life with gusto.

ON BEING JEWISH

I am Jewish, yet my sense of Jewishness is puzzling even to myself. I am historically and traditionally Jewish and religiously agnostic at best. The prayers in the temple during the High Holidays don't mean much to me. Yet, being part of the Jewish tribe means everything. I observe the major holidays by gathering my family around me and joining them in eating more than we need to. (What else do you do during holidays with family?)

Most Israeli Jews do not believe in God. They are atheists. Yet, our heritage provides such a unity, such a strong bond! We Jews relive and retell the story of our ancestors over and over again, year in and year out.

Our most famous stories of survival are represented in holidays such as Passover (when, under Moses's guidance, we were freed from Pharaoh's bondage) and Purim (the story of Haman, who tried to annihilate the Jews and perished just like his contemporary counterpart, Hitler). We recall and observe our traditions every year without religious belief. I don't believe in a deity, and yet that is part of the cultural, traditional system that binds Jews as a group. That bond is important to me. Do I make sense? Do I have to?

Looking at the whole tradition, I pick and choose what makes sense to me. I am an adult, and I've earned the right to believe what makes sense to me. I don't have to prove that I'm Jewish. I know I am.

Allow me to quote from *The World as I See It*, by Albert Einstein. He said it so well! "The pursuit of knowledge for its own sake, an almost fanatical love of justice, and the desire for personal independence—these are the features of the Jewish tradition which make me thank my lucky stars that I belong to it."

At present, we are not members of a temple. At the High Holidays we join our children in their house of worship. My children are more religious than I have ever been. Once when I asked them if they believe in God, they said, "Sure, Mother." That is very different from what I used to say to my mother. When she threw up her hands at my "misbehavior" and said, "God will punish you," I would reply to her consternation, "What God?" God was a concept I could never relate to.

Jerry's religious background is eclectic. He comes from a very idiosyncratic family. His paternal grandmother was a Christian Scientist. She thought that God creates only perfection. "There is no good or bad," she would say. "It's the way you see it." His mother was born Jewish, so he's Jewish. Growing up in Independence, Missouri, he was surrounded by Mormons. His was the only Jewish family in town. Jerry is spiritual and intrigued by religion.

Years ago we saw the Reverend Jimmy Swaggart on television. It was fascinating. We also saw the Reverend Robert Schuller and the televised Crystal Cathedral service. All those people—they can't all be fakers! Apparently they have faith. The Reverend Swaggart preached, "Now is the time; now is your moment; accept Jesus or you will go to hell." I looked at Jerry; he looked at me. "If I could accept him," I said in earnest, "I would."

Research shows that people all over the world possess a DNA component of faith. The need to believe in a deity is a widespread need. I am in the minority for sure.

Despite being agnostic, I don't have a fear of death. I have a pragmatic attitude; when it's time, it's time. When I used to think about death, the accompanying thought was, *At the end of life, I cannot breathe. I am gasping for air*, like when we were in the attic, under the hay, hiding from the Gestapo, and my mother's hand was clamped over my mouth. I do not think that anymore. I trust and I hope that when I die, I will expire quickly, peacefully, preferably in my bed in the presence of my family. Just like my parents did.

When the children were young, we were members of Temple Maarav, the Conservative temple where I taught Hebrew. Our children went to Sunday school and to Hebrew school. But the Hebrew language is difficult to learn, and Diana gave it up. She dropped out. We didn't push her because she was a girl. It wasn't so important for her to have a bat mitzvah (a religious ceremony that commemorates passage into adulthood).

Johnny had a bar mitzvah. He wanted the reward of that rite of passage. Now both of our children belong to a temple, and their children go to Hebrew school. That means they go twice a week for four years. That's a long time considering all of the lessons and activities children have these days. But it strengthens the traditions and develops a Jewish identity. Preserving our family's Jewish identity is very important to me and, I trust, to my children as well.

Distances and perspectives are different when you are a child. A few years ago, Jerry and I went to the United States Holocaust Memorial Museum in Washington, DC, and saw an exhibition of debris from the Holocaust. We saw heaps of shoes with holes. My shoes were in the pile—or they could have been. We saw the cattle cars. They seemed so small. I remembered them as large and frightening. There was a collage of pictures of camp refugees from Mogilev. I looked for myself among mass of people, but I did not find me.

I stood in front of the pictures with tears gushing down uncontrollably. Nothing specific caused my tears. In silence, I just stood there weeping, and Jerry did not know what to do with me. "I'm fine," I said. "I just need to cry." I walked ahead, away from him. I did not want to share my experience; I did not want to reassure him that I was fine. I really wanted to allow myself to emote. It had nothing to do with him.

I wandered into a room where, through headsets, you could listen to survivors telling their own horror stories.

I sat next to a woman and shared a headphone as we listened to stories of mothers stealing food from their daughters in order to survive—or the other way around. We both sobbed, sharing the experience. When the tape was finished, we stood up, did not look at each other, and continued our journey. I did not see her face.

ON HEALING

For years and years, when I was out driving, if I heard a siren, tears would gush down my cheeks. When Johnny played saxophone in the school band, we would go to his performances. Whenever I heard the drums, tears would start flowing uncontrollably. That's how it was. It must have been from my childhood memories of German military marches and sirens.

Those tears clearly came from a deeply subconscious place, because I had no feelings, no awareness, of sadness or fear. Never mind the makeup I wore or the people around me—tears flowed and flowed some more.

Then, about ten years ago, I was driving along a highway and a siren went by. No more tears. Just like that, I was healed. I was astonished. I thought it was really interesting that it can happen.

Not everyone heals. My mother had nightmares about the Germans, the Gestapo, right up to the end. She never got over it. She never was healed.

ON GENDER ROLES

I am the son my father never had. That is not to say that I was ever confused about my gender or that I did not want to be female. What I know is that I could do whatever boys could do. I could learn to swim. I could go for higher education. I was not a sissy watching the boys climbing trees. I was climbing with them, one of them, but still being a girl, a brave girl who would fall down, scrape her arm, fight the boys, and not cry. Never cry.

I've always related to men more than to women. I identify more with their thinking. To this day, the man ("Tarzan") is expected to provide for and take care of the woman ("Jane") and the little offspring. He is expected to perform in and out of bed—but especially in bed. Jane, on the other hand, is subject to lesser expectations. She can have her cake and eat it, too. At present, in America, women have made great strides in the pursuit of equality—different but equal, at least in the eyes of the law, if not 100 percent in the workplace. Equal power commands equal responsibility.

Among my peers, my views of equal partnership and shared power are not popular, to say the least. My peers and many young women of today believe it is essential to be full-time mothers at home while the children are young.

Research does not support this widely held belief that full-time homemakers are better parents than those in the workforce. Depending on job satisfaction, support with house chores, and child care, women who contribute significantly to family income reported more self-esteem and power of decision in the family than full-time homemakers.

Children will do well if they have good care while the parents are working. Then, when the parents come home, both of them can devote time to the children.

It's not the amount of time—it's the quality of time spent. I had to find out for myself that I was doing the right thing, that I'm not a bad person. A career woman pays a price. Society expects that the work is still waiting for her when she gets home. There is no reason why husbands and children can't participate in the household chores. In our household, everyone had chores. I would not have it any other way. The children did their own laundry as soon as they could reach the "on" switch.

ON RAISING CHILDREN

Which is the deciding factor shaping human development? Is it nature or nurture? Is it genetic encoding or environmental influence? The age-old debate is far from resolved. The majority opinion is that both genetics and environment contribute to the individuals we become.

In my opinion the genetic programming far outweighs the environmental influences. But despite the strong role of genetics, environmental factors such as parental influence come into play. Parenting styles differ depending on the particular culture and child-rearing practices.

In the Western Hemisphere, where we reside, the authoritarian style—"Do as I say"—and the permissive idea that "anything goes" are extremes that have moved in and out of favor over the decades.

At the present time, democratic parenting is definitely favored among educated people. The premise is that in our complex world, it is important to empower our children with negotiation skills and to give them choices that carry clear-cut consequences. Such children will become the self-reliant, empowered adults who can take responsibility for their choices and actions and become the leaders of tomorrow. The end result of effective parenting, the transmission of values from one generation to the next, stems from a complex plethora of experiences to which the child is exposed:

» Safety, trust, affection, and nurturing are essential ingredients in the process of developing wellness. It is important that parents notice and reinforce a child when he or she is showing good, desirable behavior. Distracting the child or ignoring undesirable behavior, and setting clear-cut consequences for broken rules, are essential ingredients for an effective process of socialization.

» Commitment to teaching values, setting limits, and encouraging tolerance of frustration is essential to shaping character and promoting virtues such as patience, postponement of gratification, and cooperation. "You like to catch the ball? You're very good. We're very proud of you. But you have to wait for your turn; you cannot push Jake away and take his ball just because you are stronger. It is his turn now. You would not like it if he took away your turn."

» Promote self-reliance through empowerment. That is, involve children in decisions pertaining to them and foster and expand their negotiation skills. They will learn that their choices and actions have consequences and will take responsibility for them. "Your room needs to be picked up and vacuumed. When will you do it? Before you go out to play, or after dinner in lieu of your favorite program?"

The most precious gift parents can bestow upon their kids is to steer them toward self-reliance. Do not do for a child what the child can do for himself or herself—age appropriately, of course. Feeling good about oneself is achieved through accomplishments. No task is too small for a child to experience the joy of mastery, whether that means feeding and dressing themselves as young children or doing laundry and cooking in later years. Character is taught early. While promoting the child's physical and psychological growth, it is essential to teach early on that privileges come with responsibilities.

ON BIOLOGICAL BREAKTHROUGHS

Breakthroughs in genetic research are bound to bring about amazing challenges in our modern times. With the mapping of the genetic code and manipulation of stem cells, nonhuman cloning is already happening. It is inevitable. You cannot stop building an airplane if you have figured out how to keep it in the air.

It's mind-boggling that it's possible to identify the particular gene for Down syndrome or Parkinson's disease. Yet, will the time come when an employer asks whether an employee is carrying a gene for cancer or multiple sclerosis?

And it's spooky to think of human cloning—two identical human beings created deliberately, like in the movies. To use genetics and cloning to make everyone "perfect" would soon be boring; then, what was once rejected would be desired. In China, for example, where boys were valued and girls were killed, there is now a surplus of men, and women are in demand.

Regarding sexual mores, we've gone from "everything and anything goes" back to modesty. The pendulum of social movements swings back and forth between extremes. Then nature, it seems, moves toward homeostasis—a balance.

The information explosion is truly amazing. For example, you can hold an entire computer in the palm of your hand. The thought that I won't be here to watch how it all evolves in the next generation is very frustrating. It's absolutely cruel, our shared destiny that someday we will be no more and won't see what's happening. But maybe we will self-destruct before our natural death.

Consider the dangers of weapons of mass destruction, as well as global warming and other ecological disasters. We may drown in our own mess. Yet, we cannot deny the excitement of the new. The conflict rages between the moralists trying to keep things in check and the forces of constant discovery and change. We are living in very exciting times.

ON LIFE AFTER DEATH

I don't know about reincarnation. I don't try to explain the phenomenon, if it exists. I know there is an energy that survives. Nothing is lost in this universe. We come to this life; we go back into the earth. We become fertilizer for growth of other life forms. As far as the spirit is concerned, perhaps it's an electrical phenomenon. Perhaps it's a form of light that goes forth and does its thing. So be it. I don't know about an afterlife.

Elizabeth Kübler-Ross has written a lot about death and dying, especially near-death experiences. Apparently, like a computer, we shut down when we die. We see lights and a tunnel and so forth. I recall hearing about a little boy in Israel, in Jerusalem. The story goes that before he learned to read, he knew the Bible from cover to cover and could explain the Talmud. How in the world could that be? Rather than believing he is a reincarnation of another person, perhaps DNA is passed down through generations, and this boy has a "memory" of knowledge from ancestors. We know traits are inherited. We are genetically programmed. Who knows? Such accounts definitely give one pause.

I ponder the close connections of Jews throughout the world—an amazing people. When something happens to the Jews in Ethiopia, there is a global uproar. The Jewish public all over the world comes to the rescue.

What's the big deal? We are the "People of the Book." Through thousands of years of questioning in the Talmud, a common approach has developed: "If this, then that." All of those neurological dendrite connections are part of our genetic inheritance. The centuries of discussing religion and philosophy, of composing and performing great music, of painstakingly studying the human body, the planets and the stars, could result in a collective accumulation of particular cells in our genes that influences who we are—a unique genetic code with a multitude of traits transmitted to us over generations from our ancestral roots. I cherish my entire pool of genes and am committed to carry on and transmit them to future generations.

ON LIFE'S JOURNEY: MY BELIEFS

» Life is a gift, a journey, both smooth and rocky.

» Flex your muscles of experience.

» There is no failure. Disappointments make the joy of accomplishments so much greater.

» Hurt brings opportunity for growth and healing. Cherish it all.

» Live life today. The past is gone. The future might never be.

APPENDIX

MY PERSPECTIVE: JERRY MILLER

Erica and I met on a blind date. At our first meeting, as I stood in the doorway, she asked, "What would you like to do this evening?" I suggested we go to a movie. She said, "No, I don't want to go to a movie. We can't get to know each other." Then and now, she comes straight to the point. Erica was the first Israeli I had ever met, and I wasn't used to someone being so direct. I soon learned that she spoke her mind, and I didn't have to guess where she stood. That was OK with me.

So I took her to the Mexican Village, where they had dancing—not even knowing how very much she loved to dance. It was a very nice evening and the beginning of six or seven months of dating pretty regularly, but not exclusively. One day she said (with her customary candor), "Jerry, I have good news for you. Someone else has asked me to marry him. I prefer marrying you, but I would like a decision." I said, "Well, give me two months to think about it, and I'll let you know." That was much too long for her to wait. Within a couple of weeks, we decided to get married and we set the date.

It has been a successful marriage, and we've had a lot of good fortune along the way. The only really tough times for Erica and me were during the years she was a full-time student in pursuit of her PhD and our children were young. Erica wanted to go back to school, and we had a family. She was driven to get her PhD and it was important to her. She was very determined. There was no stopping her. She did not miss a beat: four years undergraduate, two years master's, two years PhD.

It was tough for all of us. I became the mother hen. I went to parent-teacher conferences. I picked up whatever and wherever Erica could not. It was definitely a family affair. We survived the challenge and prospered. I must note that despite her demanding graduate work, she made sure that we knew family was important. We always had dinner together. Sunday was family day with grandparents, and every year we took vacations with and without our children. Those were cherished times for all of us.

I have a varied business background, which prepared me well for several ventures Erica and I have embarked on. After the Korean War, I went to USC on the G.I. Bill and after graduation went on to UCLA to get my teaching credential, which I used for a very short time. There was not enough money in teaching. Business was my calling. I was an entrepreneur. I tried many things, and Erica was always there to applaud my ventures. In my youth I dabbled in comedy writing. I would have liked to become a comedy writer. It was never to be. Instead, I followed a business route.

After she received her PhD, Erica was successful in whatever she attempted. First she worked for a clinic in Encino and soon became the preferred therapist there. Then she decided to open her own office. Erica was a good therapist, but she had no marketing knowledge. She asked me to help with the marketing aspect of the business, which I did. Our joint partnership—my marketing ability and her clinical and administrative skills—led to the establishment of a chain of successful mental health centers all over Los Angeles and Orange counties.

In 1994, I saw an advertisement for a one-hundred-unit property for sale in Austin, Texas. It was a come-on ad. Fortunately, Southwest Airlines had a two-for-one special going. I talked to the agent for that property and others, and he said, "Come on down and bring your wife." We looked at a variety of properties and deals. As we looked around, Erica saw a sixteen-unit apartment building. She asked me if the two of us should buy it or if she should buy it with her sister. She and her sister had inherited a four-unit apartment building in Los Angeles. I suggested she buy it with her sister, which they did.

Erica had a lot of foresight in recognizing opportunities. She decided to refinance the property, and she and her sister were able to increase their income very nicely with this investment. Later, we bought other properties in Texas, and we are glad we did. We pat each other on the back. I was the one who found the ad for Texas real estate, but equally important, Erica was willing to make the trip down there to check it out. A lot of people would say it was nuts to follow a shaky lead all the way to Texas, but Erica was willing to do it. She also has an eye for spotting valuable properties.

Erica has always been willing to gamble on an opportunity. If I made a decision that didn't turn out, or if I made a mistake, she never held it up to me. I have really appreciated that over the years. A person wants to hear when you're successful. You don't want people to remind you of mistakes. She has always been encouraging and supportive of my ventures. Erica is very upbeat and positive and takes advantage of opportunities that come along.

Erica is a very devoted and good mother. She was more of a disciplinarian raising the children than I was. If we had any major arguments, it was over child-rearing issues, particularly Diana. In my eyes, Diana could do no wrong. So Erica corrected her when she was out of line. Both of our children grew up to be nice human beings. Both of them graduated from UCLA and from law school. Johnny makes his living as a lawyer, and Diana is a dedicated homemaker and busy mother of three.

Our family has had a lot of good times. We enjoy our two children, both of whom are really good citizens. We have five grandchildren. All five are unique, bright, and wonderful in their own way. I enjoy playing games with them and going to their sports and other events.

Erica enjoys these activities too, although she has no interest in sports, especially American spectator sports. When she walks by the TV and sees a football game, she says, "All they do is fall down and get up." On one occasion, I persuaded her to attend a wrestling match with me and her sister and brother-in-law. She didn't know what to expect. As the wrestling commenced, she exclaimed, "I cannot believe that grown people watch this stuff!"

Erica and I come from very different family backgrounds. My grandparents are from Leavenworth, Kansas. They weren't in the slammer or anything, but they were born there. They lived in Independence, Missouri, and that's where I was raised. During the Depression, we lived with my maternal grandparents because my father was unemployed. My Jewish grandfather had a successful business—a scrap yard. He did well because the land continued to appreciate, and he would sell his property and move farther out.

My grandmother was a little different. She got involved with the Christian Science Church, and her views kind of rubbed off on my mother. Erica didn't know my grandmother and could never understand my mother. Erica had never met anyone like that. When someone was ill, my mother said she was helping him or her. "Help" to her was having a practitioner say a prayer.

Erica's parents, on the other hand, came to this country from Israel. Her father was a very bright man and spoke five languages (Rumanian, German, Russian, Hebrew, and Yiddish), but not English. He described himself as a bookkeeper, but in the United States, he would have been considered an accountant. He was very knowledgeable about accounting procedures.

Their first year in Los Angeles was really difficult. He couldn't find a job, and I spent a lot of time helping them get settled. I would find him jobs here and there, and he would lose them because of the language obstacle, among others. For example, he had never used a phone. The phone would ring and he would get very nervous. The caller would say, "Who's this?" And he would say, "Who's this? Who's this?" Not only that—when he got nervous he would lose his hearing, so he didn't last long in office jobs.

I tried to think what I could do to get him started in a business. Finally, I came up with the dry-cleaning business. I said, "Erica, cleaning is a good business. There's no inventory. We'll try it. It doesn't cost much to set it up." I didn't know that you had to take an examination to operate a cleaning establishment. I said I would take the examination.

I was given a book to read and told to go to classes. Well, I wasn't going to go to classes, but I went to the exam and took the test. It was quite difficult. I knew the answers to questions about workers' compensation, but I knew nothing about cleaning chemicals, or how many stitches there are to an inch.

I put on a pair of sunglasses and sat next to a guy who seemed to know what he was doing. I copied his answers. As I was coming out of the room, the examiner asked me to press a skirt. I had never pressed a skirt in my life, but I made a stab at it.

At home, Erica said, "How did you do on the exam?" I said I had no idea. In a few days I got the results. Honest to God, I scored about 97 on the examination and got the license. Erica was very grateful to me, and I was glad to help out. I enjoyed the challenge. Erica's parents found themselves a niche, made a living, and grew old next to their girls, and life was good.

Erica and I make a good team. Our skills are very complementary. When I generated business ideas, she would be very supportive—often jumping right in and following through. She's very good at details. I'm better with the big picture. I often bought businesses that I knew nothing about. To me, business is business. I'm skilled with marketing, and Erica can manage and implement the project or the product.

Historically, I get a business up and running, such as the wooden pallet business. Then, I often sell it and buy something else. I know I can always count on Erica to support me and encourage me in these ventures. Usually I'm successful, but if not, Erica can roll with it. She doesn't worry like I do. I'm a worrier. I worry about litigation with our apartments. Insurance can't cover everything, but it doesn't bother Erica.

Erica started out with a lot of negatives in her life— being in the camps, and the family being hunted even after that, not going to school until age twelve, and then studying in a foreign language. She's a real survivor, a high achiever and exceptionally intelligent—very, very capable. In our family, there is no one quite as assertive and successful as she is.

It's interesting—neither one of us is really retired, even though we are of "retirement age." We enjoy managing our businesses, and we share the duties in the house. Erica cooks, makes the beds, and keeps things neat. I do the dishes and the laundry. We enjoy traveling together. We go to Austin about every six weeks, where we conduct business and shop during the day and enjoy socializing in the evenings. We are never bored with each other. We argue about politics and social issues because I'm more liberal than she is.

People sometimes comment on our long marriage. I would say that a primary ingredient is having a fundamental respect for each other. Whatever I want to do, Erica always encourages me to do it, no matter how off base it might be. She never says, "You can't do it." Had I pursued my comedy writing, she would have cheered me on. I respect her intelligence and drive. I am amazed at what she has achieved, and I think I've added a lot to her life, too.

Also, it's been important to take into consideration our very different backgrounds. We both had to make allowances for each other's family members. All in all, the good aspects far outweigh the bad. We always try to work out our differences. We don't bring up past mistakes. Erica is more open than I am. She always wants to discuss things. So communication is very important, as is a sense of humor.

We've had a good life together. Erica and I have been very fortunate. Our children are doing well. Erica and I both had significant roles in their development. We are proud of them.

Life is good.

MY LIFE AS A DAUGHTER: DIANA MILLER TURK

I think this is a valuable thing to do—my mother writing her life story. It's good for me and for the grandkids later on. I'm glad to be a part of it.

My mother wants to know what it was like for me, growing up in our household. Nowadays, I'm very close to my mother. I talk to her every day—sometimes a couple of times a day. She's one of the most important people in my life, but it was not always like this between us.

I had a lot more conflict with my mother than with my dad. Growing up was hard for me—much of it having to do with my mother. There was a lot of fighting, a lot of conflict. However, compared to what I hear about other families, I think I had a good family life. My parents were together. We had a strong family. Yet, I always thought my parents would get divorced because they were so different from each other. They were just so opposite. They had a lot of conflicts—mostly my mother yelling at my father.

My father would tell me, "Your mother is crazy," affirming my experience of how difficult she was. I, too, thought she had crazy behavior. She was often very explosive—mostly at my father, my Omama (her mother), and me.

I just figured one day my dad would leave. "Why should he be treated like this?" I wondered. Although my parents clearly have a strong bond, I didn't see much demonstration of their affection. If there was any, it was from my mother to my father. My dad isn't a demonstrative person. As a kid, I thought that if they split I would go with my father because I was much closer to him and felt more loved by him. I felt that my mother didn't like me when I was growing up.

Now I understand some of the reasons my mother was so angry. She had a rough time. She wanted to be a psychologist, and I think the whole family was against her pursuing her goal. She was a full-time graduate student in a demanding PhD program, which required studying in a language (English) that was not her native tongue. She was very stressed. My dad wanted a wife who would be a mother at home, so she was fighting all of us. I think that's why she had so much anger.

Now it's so much better because she's where she wanted to be. As a child, though, I thought my dad wouldn't put up with it anymore. However, he's too nice of a guy ever to do that. I remember that sometimes I wished they would get divorced so that I could live with my dad. I didn't like living with my mother. Thank God I had my dad and my Omama, because they loved me unconditionally. My dad was very close to my mom's parents. In fact, Mom and Dad were united as caretakers of Mom's parents.

So how did I experience my mother as I was growing up? I have a mixture of happy and painful memories. My mother was constantly criticizing me. I just felt like everything I did was wrong in her eyes—that she was constantly pointing a finger at me. I felt beaten down emotionally. I took her criticisms and her anger very personally. Those experiences shaped me into the person I am today. It was very hard to take all of that anger directed at me just for being who I was. A mother is the primary person in your life as you are growing up. I felt like she didn't like me, and it hurt horribly.

Now I realize that my mother was trying to do something nobody wanted her to do. Like my dad, I wanted my mother at home. I wanted my mother to be the Brownie leader, to pick me up from school. I wanted a mother present. I was very bonded with my dad, and I think he felt bad for me. My dad and I had a very special, close relationship—kind of watching out for each other. I was also very close to my Omama, and she and my dad didn't approve of the way my mother treated me.

My mother didn't ever physically abuse me, but I felt verbally abused. I don't remember the words she used, but the tone of voice was so full of frustration. Omama was very loving and protective of me, as was my father, and I returned their deep affection. Later, when I was in college, other kids wouldn't have time for their grandparents, but I had so much time for mine. I'd visit Omama. I took her everywhere with me: school, the library, shopping, and even to aerobics. When my mother got so angry, I always felt safe because I had my Omama and my dad.

I remember that once I ran away from home and stayed with a girlfriend for a couple of days. I wanted to run away a lot of times, just because it was so hard. I didn't know who I was. Maybe part of the problem was that I was just like my father and so much the opposite of my mother. It's interesting that despite everything, I really did well in school. I was class president, and I graduated with honors. I never studied. I was just naturally gifted. Things came easily to me. I achieved a lot. Even though my mother acknowledged my achievements, it felt like she took them more or less for granted. I didn't get a lot of positive strokes.

Another interesting phenomenon is that I had so many friends. I had an abundance of really close friends, more than normal. Perhaps I needed so many friends because I felt rejection at home. Maybe I needed to get validation elsewhere.

I have a lot of happy memories, too. In elementary and junior high, my friends thought my mother was so cool because she dressed cute. There is a younger side to her than her chronological age, which I admire. I remember that when I was in sixth grade, she had jeans and a jean jacket when women were just starting to wear pants. My friends thought it was so great that I had this hip mother. That made me feel proud. She always looked fantastic. She was really with it and kept up with the styles, and I felt good about that. I was proud to show her off, and a part of me felt good that my mother was in school, studying to become a doctor. Other mothers were just at home, and she wasn't like typical mothers.

More happy memories include Sunday afternoons with my father. After Sunday school, my dad would pick up my brother and me, and we'd go to Fedco (a predecessor to Costco) and buy unhealthy food. I especially remember the fried chicken wings! My mother was kind of a health nut. She didn't let us have candy or fried chicken wings. At Fedco we also bought bagels and cream cheese for Sunday morning brunch, but fried chicken wings made my day. We threw the bones out the window as we drove home because we didn't want Mother to see that we were eating junk food.

My parents were not united at all in their opinions about child rearing. This was not good. My mother would want to punish me, and my dad would take me out for ice cream. My mother would have healthy food in the house for my lunches, and my dad would take us to 7-Eleven on the way to school and buy a couple of candy bars. Dad would say, "Don't tell mother." Looking back now, it was comical.

We went on family trips. Those were good. I really liked our trips. When my mom was away from her work and school, vacations were enjoyable. I remember loving those vacations with the family. I enjoyed spending twenty-four hours a day with my family, because we got so little of that. Things were much better with my mother on vacations. She was a lot less stressed.

My earliest memories, from when Mom was a Hebrew school teacher, are positive. She was pleasant, nice. We would get together with other families, with my cousins, both my dad's side and my mom's side. I remember when I was about six years old and was playing outside without a shirt on. The kids in the neighborhood said, "How come you're a girl and you don't have a shirt on?" And my mom said, "What's the big deal?" She was European, and in Europe even adult women go topless on the beach. The kids in the neighborhood thought I was weird because I would go topless, but my mother thought it was acceptable for a small child. Because she was foreign-born, I felt that we were a little different. I was a little bit embarrassed, because maybe she didn't know the right thing—maybe you're not supposed to go topless.

I also remember being angry early on because when the Helms Bakery truck came around, all the other kids could get doughnuts, but not us. Because my mother was a health fanatic, we couldn't have any sweets. I would see my next-door neighbor getting apple pies and doughnuts (today she's 200 pounds), and I begrudged the fact that everybody was getting these goodies but us.

The difficult times with my mother were during those eight years when she was in school—first as an undergraduate and then in the PhD program. Those years coincided with my junior high and high school years, which are very important. In my opinion, it was just too much for a person to handle—to raise a family and go to school full time and not to have support from your spouse or your children. I know I wouldn't be able to do that. When I was in law school, I could only handle being in law school. I couldn't even handle being in a relationship.

Another real plus for me was my brother, John. He was one of my best friends. John and I never fought. Today I have a hard time watching my kids fight. They are very close in age, and they fight a lot. I just can't understand it, because I hardly ever fought with John. It's funny how my son tells me, "You guys weren't normal" (because we didn't fight).

Even though he was three years younger, John and I were very close. I liked to take care of him. I've always wanted to take care of him. I consoled him and didn't talk to him about my differences with Mom. My Omama and my dad took care of me. I wanted to take care of John. I included him in everything. I just loved him. I adore him to this day. He is incredible. Compared with my friends and their siblings, John and I have the closest relationship of any I've seen, even between sisters. I talk to him every day, sometimes a couple of times. Our mother doesn't like to bother him at work, but I have no problem with that.

Growing up, I got some very clear messages from my mother. She put a lot of emphasis on achieving. Another strong message was: Women should work and have a career. Mom always disagreed with women who "stood behind" their men and didn't develop their own potential. That's probably the biggest message I got. Another message was, "MARRY JEWISH." Maybe because she is a Holocaust survivor, I've always been more attracted to Jewish people. This is all from my mother, not from my father. I got the message from my mother, "Be with Jewish people after what we've been through—after what I've been through. Marry Jewish. Surround yourself with Jews." She remembered how people had turned against her, and it could happen again. She wanted us to keep our faith, our ethnic identity. Also, she believed the more you have in common with your spouse, the more likely it is that the marriage will last.

As I was growing up, we weren't religious, but there were certain guidelines. At Passover we couldn't have bread. If my brother or I wanted to go to a football game on a Jewish holiday, we couldn't go. The traditions were important, but not so much the idea of God, or obeying God's rules or keeping kosher. It was more important to remember what the Jewish people have gone through and follow the traditions.

During college years, things weren't as bad, since I was away. But I still had a lot of anger built up from all the previous years. My mother has had a hard time with the fact that I'm not as career-oriented as she is. I went to law school and I didn't pass the bar. She wanted me to be a "little Erica," but I'm more like my father and just not as career-oriented. She had a hard time with the fact that I wasn't passionate about law. To make matters worse, when I was studying for the bar, I had to quit my job. I couldn't support myself, and she resented that I was still getting financial support from my parents.

I went to therapy during some of those stressful years, and one thing a therapist said to me, which I think was accurate, was that my mother resented the close relationship my father and I had. He wanted someone to take care of—my mother was so independent—and I allowed him to take care of me. Actually, we took care of each other, mentally and emotionally.

When I got married, things changed with my mother. Once I had a husband, my relationship with my mother got much better. For one thing, there wasn't the same struggle vis-à-vis my father. I got pregnant about four months after I got married. I began raising a child, and Mom was right in there with me.

Our relationship is much, much better now. My mom is more settled. I still have occasional fights with her, and my husband knows about those. He gets to listen to my end. She still doesn't approve of my lifestyle because I'm not in a paying career. Sometimes I feel she tries to tell me how to raise my children. If I don't want to listen to her, she'll take it personally and become upset with me. Once she didn't talk to me for two weeks. I was going to go see a therapist for one of my children. She couldn't believe that I would pay to go and see someone when my own mother is a therapist. She thought I had the best advice possible right at my own back door, but I just didn't feel she could be objective.

A lot of what she says today does not affect me the way it used to. Today I'm able to put it in perspective. I've learned to listen differently. I can take what applies and let the rest go. I listen to her, but I don't argue so much. The fighting is just not worth it for me, so we get along much better. I see that she is such a good person. She cares deeply and needs to express her opinions.

Nowadays, I'm very close to my mother. She's one of the most important people in my life. I feel very protective of her, too. On one occasion, my mom, my oldest daughter, and I went to San Francisco. I had a wonderful time. I like to be with her. I enjoy going on vacations with my parents. I go by their house frequently. It's interesting that I talk more to my mother now than to my father. She's easier to talk to at this stage of our lives, and we get into in-depth conversations and details. Maybe it's a woman-to-woman thing. My father hears me if I have a complaint or something to say, but (like most men) he just kind of brushes it off rather than getting into it.

In 2004, I took Mom to Mexico—just for the day. We went to Rosarita Beach—we left at six in the morning and came back at ten at night. I took a girlfriend, too, and the three of us spent the day together. It was very nice. We have a very positive relationship. Compared with my friends and their mothers, it's one of the closest mother-daughter relationships I know of. It's amazing how it has turned around.

Also, beginning in 2006, we started a new tradition. In January every year, when there aren't many tourists, we go to Italy for one week. We both love to travel, especially to Italy. Usually, we take one of my girlfriends with us. Mom feels like an equal to my fortysomething girlfriends, and she is. People think she is my sister, and it makes her feel great.

She relates to my girlfriends 100 percent. She loves it, and so do I. She has more energy and stamina than my girlfriends and I. It is truly amazing! I am very lucky to do this trip with her. It is one of the highlights each year.

We live close to each other and see each other often. It is seven minutes from her door to my door. I see her maybe four times a week. I might just stop in for twenty minutes or five minutes just to pick up something. She's still the same person who needs to voice her opinion, but I don't take it the same way. There's not all that anger. Although I felt that she didn't want me around while I was growing up, now it's like she can't get enough. "You mean you're stopping by for only five minutes?" she asks. Her famous saying is, "I don't get enough *alone* time with you."

There have been times since my marriage when things were difficult. One time my daughter was in the hospital for a week, and I was falling apart. There were times when I had a conflict with my husband's family or with my husband, and my mother has always been there. When I need to talk, I need to talk right then. I can call her at four in the morning and she will listen. At this stage, she's been there 100 percent for me. She has supported me in so many decisions I've made. She compliments me about the way I'm raising my kids. I enjoy spending time with her. I like to take her shopping with me. Sometimes I even prefer her company to that of a girlfriend.

My husband helps a lot. One of the reasons I was attracted to him is that he accepts me for who I am. I don't have to prove anything. I think I finally realized that I am OK the way I am. He loves me unconditionally, whether I ever work a day in my life, or whether I weigh 200 pounds. Because I have a husband who accepts me unconditionally, I have less need of my mother's approval. Now I have another life, a good life with my husband and children, and my mother's opinion is not as central as it once was.

When I had my first child, Mom was so excited. She says she's not a babysitter, but she is very connected to all three of my children. She's very devoted. She really knows them. She's not just a grandparent who hands them toys and candy. Instead, she talks to them. She asks them about their interests. Sometimes she can talk to my daughter better than I can. I like that she doesn't just buy them things but makes a real effort to interact with them, and she succeeds. I respect that a lot. Even though she doesn't babysit as much as I wish she would, she's a very good grandmother. I still love the family vacations we take. They are so special. Luckily my parents are in the financial situation where they can take us on trips. We have taken so many wonderful cruises and trips with my parents. It's been great!

I feel so fortunate that both of them are alive and in good health and that they live so close by.

Mom, I love you.

GROWING UP IN THE MILLER FAMILY: JOHN MILLER

My mom was not your normal stay-at-home mom. I remember, as a very young child, saying to her, "How come you don't stay home like other kids' moms? How come you don't bake cookies?" And she would say something like, "I'm not a baker." I remember thinking she was just doing what she was doing. She was happy with that. I questioned it, but I don't think it ever impacted me. She was the only working mom among all my friends' mothers. Even when I was four or five, she was teaching Hebrew school and working just like my dad. When I was in elementary school, she went back to school, and I was always very proud of her.

I was very lucky I had my sister, Diana, who was an incredible sister-friend. She was older and always watched out for me. I never felt like I was alone. She always included me. I remember our relationship as being only positive, without sibling rivalry. Of course there were the small conflicts—"She took my Pop-Tart!"—but nothing more than that. Diana was truly phenomenal.

I don't remember ever going without because mom was away. Yet, I was probably a mama's boy. I loved her dearly and always wanted to be with her. I told her I wanted to marry her. I just couldn't get enough. I knew she had a lot of affection for me, too. She tells me that at one point she was concerned about my being too much of a mama's boy and pushed me away. (Now, when she says I'm not affectionate enough, I just blame her!)

I don't remember her pushing me away. It wasn't part of my experience. I also felt affection from my dad, in a different way, and I'm a lot like him. He is extremely easygoing and just wants to please everybody, but doesn't have to put a lot of effort into it. Pleasing people just comes naturally to him.

I think about the combination of how we four pegs fit into the square of the family. I was fortunate that I was influenced by the good parts from everybody. Truly, I can think of only good things from my childhood. I remember birthday parties, the houses we lived in, having lots of friends, and always playing outside.

I was aware that my mom and my sister had a lot of conflicts. I tried to be neutral, because I saw what could happen if I took a position against my mother. "Who needs that?" I thought. "Not me." Occasionally I tried to mediate, but mainly I just stayed out of the conflict. I would tell my sister to let the yelling go in one ear and out the other. As an adult, I mediate more often.

What was my dad's position in all this? He just wanted everyone to be happy, so he tried to be a peacemaker in the most gingerly way possible. If one of them got mad at him, he wouldn't allow himself to get engaged. He would generally drop it.

My dad took on a lot of nontraditional dad roles when I was very young, because Mom was working and going to school. He would take Diana and me to McDonald's or somewhere because Mom was at school or studying. I learned to do my own laundry at a very early age.

As I said, Mom's being gone a lot didn't impact me, but with Diana, it was a different story. She always felt that mom's juggling act caused a lot of stress that impacted her. I never felt that. Maybe it's genetic—different ways the mind works. I don't know. My sister and I laugh, "Did we grow up in the same house?"

My sister and I had babysitters galore—from after school until six o'clock or so. A lot of them were high school kids from the neighborhood. I saw my friends' parents a lot and was in and out of their homes. It was like a village because we were a part of so many families in our neighborhood.

I remember especially the neighbors across the street: Louise Carroway and her husband, Wayne. Mrs. Carroway was also our piano teacher when I was about five. I felt like we lived at her house. We spent a lot of time there. The funny thing was, she was completely different from us. She was a born-again Christian, always displaying her Christian values. Although they were 180 degrees different from us, they were like family. Their beliefs didn't really concern me, but I always wanted a Christmas tree.

My grandmother on my dad's side was an important adult in my life. Her name was Ruth. She was always a riot, I thought. She was definitely a Midwesterner—a product of five generations of settlers in Kansas and Missouri. My mother called her an "Okie." She was a wonderful grandmother to my sister and me. We slept over at her house frequently on weekends. We just loved going over there, just loved it. She took us to marionette shows at Griffith Park. In the kitchen, we baked things together, and she let us eat whatever we wanted. We played croquet in her front yard.

She was just a great traditional grandma. I always thought she was kind of funny in a quirky way, a free spirit—a little like my sister. She would do impulsive things. Grandma would get an idea about going somewhere, and we would just pack up and go. "I just made some fried chicken," she'd say, "and we're going to Knott's Berry Farm." It was great fun. I really enjoyed her. She had a husband (who was not my dad's father) with whom I never spoke. I don't remember ever saying more than two words to him. But it was fine; he was never in the way. I don't recall, but I think they actually got divorced or he died in the early 1980s.

My dad's sister, Elaine, has three kids, Mike, Debbie, and Jeff. Early in their kids' lives they lived in Las Vegas, then moved to Los Angeles for about eight years and then moved back to Las Vegas. The middle cousin, Debbie, and I were very close. She would do a lot of things with Grandma and us. Once or twice a year, we would all go to Las Vegas, and Grandma would join us there. Debbie, Diana, and I would have a great time together in Vegas. I think my mother disagreed in some ways with Grandma, possibly an in-law thing. I think both my dad and my grandmother had good traits. They really liked people and they enjoyed having a lot of friends around. I think I've emulated those traits.

Then there were my mom's parents, Omama and Opapa. Omama had a heart of gold. She didn't speak great English. German was her native tongue. She was a passive woman but had a huge heart. She stayed with us a lot. I remember she made dill pickles, stuffed cabbage, and all kinds of good things that no one makes anymore. We used to have a great time making fun of her English. She took it in good humor. She was just happy to be along. Opapa didn't have a huge impact. He was a little more formal, more distant.

My mother and I had some great times together when she would occasionally walk me to school. She was very supportive of whatever I did. I wasn't good in sports, which was a big deal at age seven or eight. At that time, if you weren't into sports, you got picked on. You were the last one chosen for teams. She told me that as I got older and taller, I would be better at sports. She said that not everyone is good at the same things and pointed out that I was good at other things. She was always a big comfort to me.

I was rarely disciplined. I'm not sure why; I certainly wasn't a perfect child. My mother was studying to be a psychologist when I was in first grade, so I don't know what child-rearing practices were in vogue. Nowadays, there's a lot of emphasis on "time-outs." A lot of my friends were spanked. I was never spanked. I was never physically disciplined. (Maybe that's why they call me a spoiled brat now.) I just remember getting a whole lot of affection. I remember my mom as always being incredibly supportive, which gave me confidence.

Some of my friends feel that their parents constantly judged them. I never felt that way. I only felt encouragement, from my dad, too. Now, as a parent, I see that encouragement and support are very important. I try to bring some of those traits to my parenting style. My mom always wanted to talk things through. As a kid, I didn't particularly want to talk. She would just say, "Listen," and I wouldn't have to respond—she'd just continue talking. What she said always made sense, and I felt comforted by her. There were times when I thought it would be nice to have her at home, but I didn't think much about it at the time. That's just how it was. As an adult I can say it was the quality of the time rather than quantity that made the difference for me.

Sometimes my mom and dad had major fights in front of Diana and me. It wasn't often, but there would be a lot of shouting and screaming. I don't remember what the specific issues were, but generally it was about juggling time between school and family. Some of her classes were at night. It was hard because my dad worked, and he had major responsibilities then as the breadwinner. But he also had to take over at home—to care for us with dinner and homework and take us to various practices and school activities. Today, my parents are very much in sync, but back then they were 180 degrees apart.

Dad came from a very traditional Midwest family. My grandmother never worked. She raised the chickens, fed the kids—Americana, a Doris Day kind of life—whereas for my mom, that was not her thing at all. She didn't like to cook. She didn't like to bake. She didn't sew. She wasn't the kind of gal who was going to sit around and wait on the family. My dad accepted that because she had a lot of other things he really liked, but tensions would arise. Diana and I would say, "They're going to get divorced."

I worried about that. We both did, especially after two or three of those huge fights erupted in front of us. My sister was truly upset and cried. There weren't a lot of those episodes, but they scared us (I think I was eight or nine at the time). Overall, I didn't get the brunt of mom's stress, so I didn't notice it. I was just a kid.

Once she got her PhD, things felt a little different. I can imagine that until she accomplished her goal, she never knew for sure she'd make it. When she graduated, everyone was so proud, truly proud. We had a great party for her. Then she started earning money, and I'm sure that eased some of the financial pressures.

Early on, she ventured out to start her own practice, Miller Psychological Centers. My dad, being entrepreneurial and having been involved in several businesses, provided the business expertise. The two of them really worked as a team. I could never do it. I think it would be tough to work with a spouse because there would never be any separation of work and home, but my parents really complemented each other. They had healthy arguments about business issues. When Mom got going in her practice, the changes were all positive for the family. Although she still was not around a lot, I was not affected by it. There were times when she did her best to be there, when I was in a play or had a band concert. Same with my dad, but he was always more available.

Even though I was proud of what my mother was doing, I was often embarrassed by her comments and by how outspoken she was, especially in front of my friends. Whenever I was going to introduce her to one of my friends, I wanted to say to her, "Don't say anything embarrassing!" But she gets mad when I say that. She's not passive or shy. She speaks her mind, so sometimes she says things that truly horrify me.

One episode stands out. My best friend growing up was Paul Minor, who lived nearby. Even at a young age, he was anti-Semitic. The area I grew up in had very few Jews. These kids were just ignorant. They didn't know any better. They'd hear comments from their parents and pick it up. The family was as "Waspy" as you could imagine. When we were eight or nine, he would make Jew jokes. Personally, I didn't care. I would just say, "You are so stupid. You don't know anything." That was that. It didn't bother me. When I mentioned it to my mom, she went ballistic, just as I would do now, as a parent.

I was out of school for Rosh Hashanah, I think. We were all getting out of our car after temple, and Paul came riding by on his bike. Paul said, "Hey, how come you weren't at school today?" I said, "Oh, it is Rosh Hashanah. We were at temple." Then he made some kind of smart remark about Jews, and Mom really lost it. She lit into him. "Listen, you." she shouted. "We're tired of your condescending remarks about Jews. You are no longer going to be Johnny's friend if you keep this up. This is unacceptable." She really read him the riot act, this little nine-year-old kid. Of course, he told all of our friends. She meant well, but I was mortified.

Mom puts her foot in her mouth frequently. We talk a lot. She likes to know what's happening with us and with our friends. Then sometimes she'll just blurt out something rather personal. She doesn't mean to. It's just that there are no secrets with her, no holding back. She loves our friends and they love her. She likes hanging out with them. She's young at heart—she thinks she's still thirty-nine! Sometimes, though, she just doesn't think before speaking. I have to watch her!

I was proud of my mom and my dad regarding vacations. They always made sure we took fun family trips. Every year we went on a phenomenal family excursion. We drove across the country—to the Wisconsin Dells, Mackinac Island in Michigan, Colorado Springs—all over. These were driving trips, up to three weeks with all four of us in the car. Every year. Phenomenal. My sister and I sat in the backseat, playing games, eating sunflower seeds, and munching on brownies Mom baked from a Betty Crocker mix. We went on cruises, and once to Hong Kong.

We were not wealthy. My parents didn't have a lot of money

until we were older. Growing up, money was always an issue. When we went to restaurants, the instructions were, "No one order anything from this side." Money was tight. It wasn't a huge issue, but my sister and I knew not to be excessive. The one thing we always did, no matter what, was to take a really nice vacation every year. That was a priority for my parents, rather than buying clothes or expensive furniture.

Now, as a parent, I am amazed they would do that every year, often for two or three weeks. For me, just taking a week off requires loads of scheduling, but we enjoyed these vacations right up through college. Even now, they take us on trips. I think it's the greatest thing to have that quality family time together. My wife, Gail, laughs at me. She thinks we are the Ozzie and Harriet of Los Angeles and that my family is like the Nelsons. I don't recall any fights on those trips—just fun, fun, fun. On vacation, my parents catered to my sister and me. Even to this day, it's fun. When we get together, we say, "Remember when we went to the Wisconsin Dells? Remember when we were in Florida and I got sick?" Those memories are awesome, memories about life. To me, they are milestones, like our trip to Vancouver, whereas my seventh birthday party I can't even remember.

Now that I'm a parent, I am so concerned about things like homework and my kids' attending the best possible school. I don't recall my parents making a big deal about such things at all. They just plopped me at the local elementary school. I don't know how

I made it through sixth grade. Today, our friends are all neurotic about the schools, finding additional outside stimulating classes, and constantly looking for enrichment activities. We didn't have any outside enrichment, except piano lessons from our neighbor across the street. That was it.

I went to Hebrew school, but I didn't like it at all. It was weird. It may be different now. I lived in an area that wasn't Jewish at all. None of my friends were Jewish, and our temple was pretty far away, in Northridge. I only saw these people from the temple twice a week. I had no Jewish friends outside the temple. My Hebrew school classmates all knew one another, as did their parents. My parents were outside the loop. There was no connection. I didn't like it, but my parents just said, "You're going. You need to have a bar mitzvah," and that was all there was to it. Since we weren't connected to the temple and none of my friends were there, it wasn't a very positive experience. Now we belong to a temple where a lot of our friends attend. We are friends with other parents, so it is more of a community.

Healthy food was an issue with my mother; again, that was not a popular thing at the time. I was a chubby kid my whole young life, even through most of high school. My mom insisted on no junk food in the house. No cookies, Ding Dongs, or chips, except on very rare occasions, such as birthday parties and vacations. Instead she offered us carrot sticks, sunflower seeds, and dehydrated apple snacks. She cooked the whole week's meals on

Sunday (sometimes Omama came over and helped) and put them in the freezer. I remember the packages, labeled Sunday, Monday, Tuesday, and so forth.

At dinnertime, when she wasn't there, we would check out the meal for that day. If we didn't like it, Dad would take us to Sizzler or Bob's Big Boy. We'd get either the fried chicken combo or the burger and fries combo and a chocolate milk shake. My sister and I and our dad (who has a sweet tooth) would do everything in our power to sneak food into the house. When I went to the homes of my friends, I was like a maniac with all of the cookies and junk food. They didn't care much because they had it all the time. Dad was our co-conspirator. He would take us to the 7-Eleven on the way to school, and we would buy Doritos or a Twinkie.

A tradition on Sundays was to go to Western Bagel to pick up bagels and then over to Fedco for cream cheese and lox and, most important, their incredible fried chicken wings. As Diana said, we would eat fried chicken wings all the way home and throw the bones out the window. Dad was right in there with us, munching away. It was a riot. At one point, Mom actually became a vegetarian. She still cooked chicken for us, but not without guilt. "I've seen the films," she'd say. "They're disgusting. It's terrible how they kill these creatures." Now, Gail and I are health food nuts, too.

The messages I got from my mother had to do with being Jewish, rather than being religious. We had Passover seders with our relatives every year, and my mom ran them. She was the Hebrew school teacher and had all the background. My dad knew very little. I'm glad my parents never caved in and got me a Christmas tree. I'd beg every year, and for an Easter basket, too. I never got either (how mean they were!). My mom was very clear that I had to marry Jewish or she would never talk to me again (so to speak). The message was that I am Jewish, that's my title, and that's how it is.

Pursuing education and achievement were also strong positive messages. She and I were going to school at the same time: studying, taking tests, getting good grades, and reaching the next level. I was very focused on grades, even as a young boy. I remember in first grade, specifically, we were put in special math and spelling groups. Teachers said they did it by colors, but I knew it was based on ability. Because my mom was studying for a career, I thought about what I wanted to be as an adult. I was always a good student and conscientious about achieving because I saw it firsthand, rather than being lectured or having discussions about it.

When I was in high school, we moved to Woodland Hills, which was one of the best things that ever happened to me. In the previous school, I had been mugged in the locker room. The neighborhood had completely turned in a matter of six or seven years. My parents immediately said, "We're moving." They did it for me. Diana was already or nearly in college. My new school was at least 50 percent Jewish. I felt at home with my friends for the first time. I felt comfortable. This was where I belonged. Even though I had good friends in grade school and junior high, I never felt like I connected on a really personal level. After a semester at the new high school, I felt so comfortable. It wasn't that my new friends were religious or were studying the Torah, but we were culturally the same.

This change was huge for me, the most important decision my parents made all through my growing-up years. In college I joined a Jewish fraternity along with friends from high school. That high school setting had a huge impact, because the old neighborhood just wasn't me at all. Recently, a couple from my junior high class contacted me. We got together and I heard what everyone was doing and what became of that group of friends. None of them went to college. They worked for companies like UPS or were managers at Toys"R"Us. It was interesting to hear, but I knew why I hadn't connected. I wonder how my life would have been had I stayed in that high school.

My mother has had a lot of impact on the decisions I have made both as a young person and as an adult, such as where to go to college, what career to pursue, and how to handle major turning points. I always have known that she's smart (my dad is, too), and I've always sought their guidance, even to this day. What my mom said always has had a big impact on me. I have always run big decisions by her, and I put a lot of weight on her opinions and value her wisdom. Sometimes I have disagreed and have told her that I heard her but needed to take a different course. I listened to her about college, career, and even buying our house. It's not that I need her approval, but I value her opinion. She has a lot to offer, and if I disagree with her, I can tell her so and go my own way.

Becoming a lawyer, however, was largely due to my sister's influence. Diana was involved in school government, so when she ran for office in high school, I ran for office in junior high. She often laid the foundation for things I would do. She went to UCLA; I did also. She went to law school; I did, too. My mother actually wanted me to be a psychologist, but no way. I had no interest in doing that. I knew she was proud that I became a lawyer. I remember seeing the newsletter she put out for the staff of Miller Psychological Centers. Somehow there was always an item in there about me. For example, "Here is a copy of my son's new business card," or "My son, Johnny, just won his first big case."

But I have to say that as adults, Mom and I have had some major fights when we have disagreed. I can barely remember what the issues were now. My sister and I have this phrase regarding Mom: "Who's in the doghouse?" "No, you talk to her because I'm in the doghouse." We've had more disagreements in the past seven years than ever before. Mom says it's because I'm not caring enough. As my life has become more complicated, as I've married, started a family, and become more involved in work, she claims I've started taking her and Dad for granted. I don't call often enough. I don't ask how they are doing. I just call to ask their opinion or get information. Those issues have been the most contentious parts of our relationship. Sometimes she doesn't speak to me for a week and others have to mediate, but other members of the family also take their turns being in the doghouse.

Mom says I've gotten better since I have had children and understand how important the parent-child relationship is. But she still feels I don't make enough time for just the two of us to get together. Along those lines, there was a blowup when Gail got a job in Washington, DC, and we moved there for a while. When Gail was working on the 1996 Democratic presidential campaign in California, we didn't tell Mom that if Clinton were re-elected, Gail would get a job in the new administration. We wanted to spare her being in a stew for a long time.

When we told her about the job offer with Donna Shalala, Clinton's secretary of health and human services, and that we were moving to Washington temporarily, she was very upset. She didn't speak to me for a long time, but she finally came to terms with it when we were moving. She says she was most upset that we had kept it from her, that I had not told her earlier. I'm sure her reaction would not have been much different.

Since our sons were born, things for her are better and worse, she says. She has less time with me alone. She is clear that she is not great with little kids. Some of our friends' parents beg to babysit for their grandchildren. Mom does not want to babysit. She loves the grandchildren dearly, but she is not comfortable one-on-one with them. Mainly they see her when we have family gatherings.

I make a real effort to call Mom more often, and things have improved in that regard. It's a work in progress, and I've learned to take differences in stride. Even as a child, I think that maybe I was an old soul and could let things roll off and not always take Mom's comments too seriously. I think I've picked up an attitude of acceptance from my dad, too. He was a saint. I don't think very many men could have made the adjustments he has made. He set the tone and always maintained a sense of humor. Even though Mom can be difficult, she's who she is and we love her. Now, as adults, we can sometimes agree to disagree. I have my dad's ability to accept difficulties and to be easygoing, and that helps.

Gail is also very career-focused. I think I learned, from dealing with my mom, that it's important for a person to do what is important to him or her. So I understand Gail's need to pursue a demanding professional career, even though it means I have to pick up a lot of the work here at home. I did my own laundry when I was in elementary school. Now, around here, I'm the cleaner. I do the dishes. I do all the laundry. I clean up. Gail, like my mom, works very hard at her career and has no interest in housework. Like my dad, I make our lunches. With a lot of our friends, the wife has quit her job to be at home. A lot of the guys grew up that way and expect it. My choice would not be that—maybe because it's not what I'm used to. My dad didn't grow up with the role he adopted at home, which makes his adjustment all the more remarkable.

I already know what my mom's tombstone is going to say: "I Was the Hit." She loves to be onstage. Once they were at a party, at a wedding. She was wearing this dress that she loves. She was working the tables. I said later, "How was the wedding, Mom? What about the bride?" She replied, "Oh, I don't know, but I was the hit." She just loves life. She loves things to be about her. I laugh. I just roll with it. It's just who she is.

I have one hot mama!

A TRANSLATION OF PAPA'S JOURNAL

Emmanuel (Mendy) Gelber, Erica Miller's father, documented his experiences before and during World War II in a journal that he started after the war was over. This account has been translated from German.

The Hitler era was a time when basic human rights were withheld from the Jews. The goal was to exterminate innocent people—men, women, children, young, and old alike—and to plunder their possessions. That was the Nazi agenda. This was a spectacle of the most inhumane treatment imaginable, perpetrated, shockingly, by one of the most cultured societies in the Western world, Germany. No child should have to see such degradation of his parents or others.

I look back to one particular day in August of 1941 when it was warm and sunny outside, but inside I felt as if a cold shower were pouring over my heart as a freezing fear gripped my chest and throat. An eerie silence followed the recent retreat of Russians, and in the presence of the German-Rumanian soldiers who remained behind, everyone wondered, "What now? Is this the calm before the storm?"

A dreadful anticipation induced feelings of abandonment. We were starkly alone in what would soon become our darkest hour. We knew something terrible was about to occur, but what specifically was going to happen to us was unknown and terrifying.

It did not take long before units of Rumanian soldiers escorted by German soldiers walked into Tshernovitz. We heard sporadic shots of gunfire. Many of our fellow Jewish citizens were killed immediately, which we learned about later. One of the first orders issued by the new Rumanian regime, headed by President Antonescu, was to establish ghettos in certain areas of the city. Soldiers stormed into people's homes, shouting, "Schmutzige Juden, heraus! Heraus!" ("Filthy Jews, get out, get out!")

Jews were driven out of their homes, forced to leave without their belongings; their properties and possessions were confiscated. Jews were herded into designated areas of the city, crowded together like cattle. Because our family home in Tshernovitz on Dobrogea 1, formerly Morgenbessergasse, was already part of the designated ghetto, fortunately, we did not have to leave our home at that time.

Simultaneously, a decree also came down from the authorities that every Jew must wear a yellow star on the left side in order to be easily identified. Verbal orders like this came from above and spread through the community. No written orders were distributed, perhaps to avoid future incriminating evidence. Nothing was written down as though this was a premeditated act to avoid leaving any records.

The nightmare intensified: plundering, burning, and vandalizing of synagogues; merciless torturing of old and young alike. Rabbi Marks and many other important people in Tshernovitz were forced to dig their own graves—their only crime being that they were Jews. The goal was obvious: Take away all of the important people, and the helplessness, the terrorizing effect on morale, could only be imagined.

We hid in our attic when we heard the soldiers approach and prayed to God to be spared a Gestapo visit. After three or four days in hiding, there would be silence, and we dared go out on the streets again with a book under our arm, trying to cover up the yellow star. We looked for Christian friends for help, people who might have some influence. But as it turned out, our only salvation came from the Jews the Germans needed for work. They were the only ones who seemed to be spared.

Because I had worked for the Russians from May 1940 to July 1941, I was put on the black list. A former Christian colleague and friend warned me to quickly disappear. Hearing that the Gestapo was after me, I decided that being deported was the safer way to go. If we continued to hide, it would only be a matter of time.

Not knowing what would happen next, in November of 1941 I made the decision to voluntarily go to the trains, which were deporting thousands of Jews. The rest of our extended family— Oskar, Joseph, and Leo—stayed behind. They had permits in writing to stay and work in the family steel factory.

It was night when our train arrived at Ataki, on the shore of the Dniester River. The dark clouds in the sky matched the mood of the people. A cold rain saturated our clothes and our few belongings. Mothers tried to comfort their hungry, crying, and fearful children. The children and elderly sobbed softly. All around us, there was nothing but wailing and despair. "Dante's Inferno" could not describe it better. Like cattle, we were beaten with no mercy and driven out of the train. We were thrown to the ground as the perpetrators yelled, "Filthy Jews." I was saved from severe injury because I was wearing layers of clothing.

People were lined up in small boats to cross the Dniester River. My nerves were shattered. I handed the officials my gold watch, pleading for my life. After a few hours on the boat, we docked and disembarked. They lined us up and marched us briskly for about an hour. At our destination, a Rumanian lieutenant sat at a long table, looking at our documents, and took away the few belongings we had left. This was official robbery.

We were now without a home. We ceased to be individuals, or even people. We were a mass with no standing, at the mercy of murderous-looking captors. We were once again herded to barracks, where German soldiers conducted body searches, looking for lice or contagious disease. What irony! With German precision, they counted every man, woman, and child in order to be able to accurately report the exact number of deportees to their supervisors. Order must prevail.

When we arrived at the center of town, it was already dark. A fine rain soaked us to the bone. We shook, not only from the wet and cold, but because we were scared. Tired, we dragged our feet through the muddy, wet streets toward our unknown destination. Suddenly, a rumor spread that we were not staying in the town but were being sent far away, to villages and farms away from civilization. This news was terrifying. People tried to slip out of the line and hide. Only a few survived because of the keen, watchful eyes of the gendarmes (soldiers). Like a miracle (because of the cover of darkness), a few of us and our families were able to lie flat on the ground next to the road while the line moved on ahead and out of sight. We lay perfectly still, one with the ground.

Our faces were covered with mud, and our clothes and shoes were drenched. After the line moved out of sight, our only thought was to find shelter for the night. A soft light in the distance drew us like moths to a flame. I knocked timidly at the door. After a long wait, the door opened a crack, and a middle-aged man peered through. In a stone-cold voice he asked, "What do you want?" I whispered, "Please, sir, give us shelter. My wife is freezing; my children are wet and hungry. Please have mercy." After I offered him the few rubles I had left, he let us in.

Once inside, we found about twenty-five other refugees sharing a small space. Every corner was taken; there was barely room for the four of us. Mother took charge; she stripped off the wet clothes from the shivering children and hung them close to a weak fire. She found a spot on a table where they could sleep. She and I lay on the damp floor. I recall the horrendous night. My thinking became confused and I started to hallucinate. The small flickering light in that room became like a fireball; I saw visions of green palms and crested clear waters. I don't know if it was seconds, minutes, or hours later that I woke up abruptly and saw the haggard faces of my wife and children, dressed in their filthy clothes, ready to move on, again into the unknown.

By early dawn, we were on the road again, dragging our wounded feet and holding on to each other as we joined a stream of other refugees, also with grim and ashen faces. The fear of being caught by the soldiers or police became secondary to the hunger pains we felt. Finally, I was able to buy bread and milk as we entered Mogilev.

News spread like wildfire—good and bad. We learned from an acquaintance that there was an empty building on Palparsia Street. We rushed over and found other families already encamped—twenty people in one room. Our arrival was not welcome. An already crowded place became even more crowded. It was a very tense coexistence. Every little family unit tried to claim a spot. Some had jewelry or clothing left that could be traded for food from the local peasants who swarmed around us like bees to honey. Some had nothing left to trade and looked hungrily at those who found something to put in their mouths.

The nervous tension continued, but after people got to know

one another, a thin veneer of kinship developed among all of us having to share the same destiny. Water was distributed sparingly. The biggest problem was lack of cleanliness or sanitation. The filth contributed to a severe outbreak of typhoid everywhere. Like a miracle, all the inhabitants of our dwelling were spared.

After a time we were moved by the local administration to one small room in a house within the ghetto. From our one tiny window, we saw carriages go by daily, piled with dead bodies.

To control the typhoid epidemic, the soldiers in charge rounded up the elderly, the distraught, and the children and sent them off to faraway villages. Mogilev was overcrowded. Scazinetz was the name of one of the outlying villages where some people were sent. Cut off from any form of contact or help, an attempt to send clothing, food, and medication—sponsored by a Jewish organization, the Bucharest Joint Community Distribution— proved fruitless. This organization arrived in Mogilev with supplies, but none of it got to the villages.

A soup and bread kitchen was established in Mogilev, but the sick and elderly still perished like flies. Weak, skeletonlike people from the outlying villages, such as Scanizetz, sneaked into Mogilev looking for food, only to be driven out and summarily shot if they didn't move fast enough.

I'll never forget one particular distant relative whose two little girls were dying. He heard about us and knocked on our door for shelter. There was no room, but I talked the owners of the house into letting them stay on the veranda. By that time, the camp residents were able to organize in order to take care of each other. As such, I was able to get the little girls to the hospital. Unfortunately, two or three days later, the girls died. I'll never forget this man stumbling back to us to tell his wife. I don't know what happened to them. There were thousands of such cases.

The Rumanian ghetto administration allowed Jews to manage their own lives. Michael Danilov, one of the refugee lawyers, was in charge, so he had some liberties. After the war, he was accused of being a traitor but then released. He didn't have a choice; he did what he could. He set up various departments, including one to register everyone and keep an account of the people.

The lawyers among us were given permission to set up a court to settle disputes. A Rumanian Jew, Buturogra, also had responsibilities within the camp. He was in charge of finding Ukrainian Jews to send away, making more room for others. Some refugees were rounded up by the police to work for the Germans. Most of those who were sent to German work camps never returned.

In May 1944, grateful to have our lives spared, my wife, two daughters (Erica and Dita) and I began our longed-for journey home, from Mogilev to Tshernovitz. In the words of a German poet, "Ich glaubte ich ertrage es nicht und habe es doch ertragen. Doch fragt nicht wie." ("I believed I could not survive this, and I indeed survived, but do not ask me how.")

EXCERPTS FROM DITA'S SHOAH INTERVIEW

I was four years old when Erica was born. She was a frail and sickly little girl who threw horrible tantrums. Perhaps that's why our mother always gave in to Erica's whims—to keep her quiet. Erica always got what she wanted.

As a child, I resented her. She was a little pest—no different from all little sisters. Erica always wanted to hang out with my friends and me. I resented that and didn't really want her around. As teenagers, our relationship was virtually nonexistent. I left home at sixteen years old and immigrated to Israel when I was seventeen, so we were separated during those formative years. Shortly after arriving in Israel, I married and started a family. As a newlywed, life was difficult in Israel. My husband and I lived in a small apartment with my in-laws during our first seven years of marriage.

I was very happy when Erica and my parents were finally able to join me in Israel three years [after I moved there]. It was obvious that Erica had grown up since the last time I'd seen her. By that time I had a son and a daughter (after immigrating to the

U.S., I had another son). When Erica first arrived in Israel, she went to live and work on a kibbutz. She had a very busy life, and we weren't able to communicate very much during that time.

Erica was always much closer to my parents than I because she lived with them longer—longer in Rumania and, after her time on the kibbutz, longer in Israel. She lived with them while she worked and went to school, which was until she was in her early twenties.

My husband, Israel, our children, and I followed my mother-in-law when she moved to Los Angeles. It was the same for Erica. She came for a visit. Her plan was to stay a few months and return to Israel. She felt it was her duty to return, but she never moved back. When Erica came to Los Angeles, she lived with us for a while. I was happy to have her here and wanted her to stay in the U.S. In part, that's why we engaged the services of a matchmaker. We wanted Erica to find a husband. Erica met lots of men through the matchmaker, but she met her husband, Jerry, through an acquaintance.

Over time, the relationship between Erica and me evolved, and we became very close while living together. At her wedding, I gave Erica away, and my husband's family was instrumental in planning the wedding. Then, when Erica started a family of her own and my parents immigrated to Los Angeles, we became even closer.

Erica is a wonderful sister. She is a very caring person, a devoted and loyal person. Family means everything to her. Of course, she expects the same devotion from family members.

Erica was close to both of our parents while growing up. In later years, however, her relationship with our father became tainted when she discovered he had inappropriate contact with her children and mine. She was furious. She confronted our father and threatened to call the police if he ever misbehaved again. I don't think he ever did again, yet I didn't speak to our father for a very long time.

I think Erica's marriage to Jerry is a dedicated one. They are good partners. Erica has a strong personality, and she can be controlling and opinionated. Jerry is smart and interesting, but I don't think the relationship has always been easy for him.

Erica is a devoted and influential mother, especially with Diana. This might not have been obvious to everyone because Erica was in school when her children were growing up. Jerry was involved with the kids in the mornings, getting them ready for school when Erica was working or going to school. Jerry, our parents, and babysitters helped out with the children so that Erica could pursue her goals. I know it meant a lot to Erica that everyone wanted to help out.

As an adult, I have always been very proud of Erica. She is very ambitious and driven, which I am not. I appreciated what Erica was trying to do. I knew it wasn't easy for her, but she never had any misgivings. Whatever she achieved, she accomplished by herself. There aren't many women in our generation able to do what she did. She can do anything she puts her mind to.

Erica is an amazing person to have achieved so much in her education, family life, and business. She came out of the ashes of the camps and prospered. She was driven. I think she is unique to have endured *and* remained committed to her goals and still to have been true to herself. She is very dedicated and accomplished.

When I came to Los Angeles, we weren't wealthy. My husband worked in maintenance and then became a plumber. I worked, too, in order to help out. I worked as a waitress in the evenings so I could be home with children during the day. This was so different from the way Erica led her life.

Like Erica, I love to travel. My husband and I did a lot of that when he was well. Now that he can't do it anymore, I feel blessed to travel with Erica and Jerry.

Erica has been a tremendous source of support to me. I've had a turbulent, stressful life, especially since my husband developed Alzheimer's. Erica was, and continues to be, a great source of comfort. Her professional wisdom about human nature is invaluable. She is like a teacher helping me to understand people and relationships, and I try to live by what she teaches me. Everyone Erica comes in contact with is crazy about her. They like to be around her, and because I am her sister, her friends accept and include me, too. Sometimes life does come full circle, despite the fact that I didn't want her around when we were kids.

Erica has a very hopeful and positive outlook on life.

She lives every day as if it's the last. She says, "Why not?

We're here, so why shouldn't we experience it all—joy and tragedy?" Because of Erica, I've also learned to accept that which we cannot change.

Sometimes I feel sad and deprived. Although I have three children and six grandchildren, I rarely see my grandchildren. When I talk with my friends, they say this is normal. They have their own lives. My son also says your children grow up with you but your grandchildren don't. It's no wonder I am closer to my children than to my grandchildren. Also, I feel lonely without my husband. When I am sad, Erica says, "Why not you? Others have gone through this, too. Make the best of it. Accept it." Erica is always there for me.

LETTER TO MY FIRST GRANDCHILD

Dear Shayna,

This is 1994. You are two years old, and I, your "Bubbe," am embarking on an exciting journey of recording my thoughts about our relationship as I experience it—thoughts, feelings, or anything else I might choose.

I want you to know that I never thought I had it in me to feel so passionate about a baby! I hate to admit it, but it is true. I do not remember being so smitten with your mom or Uncle Johnny when they were babies. That was a long time ago. I was busy getting my degree, and time passed. They were babies no more. They grew up without me noticing.

Not with you, my love. I started bonding with you when you still were in your mother's womb. Your mom named you Shayna way before your birth. I used to pat your mother's stomach, talk to you, and watch you kick. You were an active little fetus! You kicked and kicked until you were good and ready to join us. I do not think you remember (ha-ha), but you gave your mom a real hard time. You were so big (I am not sure how much you weighed, but I know it was over nine pounds) that your head could not get through the "normal" channel, I mean the vagina, and they had to lift your chunky self out the "other" way, the caesarian way. I want you to know that I was outside your mother's door (they would not let me watch your arrival; one person—your dad—was the only one permitted) waiting for your arrival.

When I first held you in my arms—I swear I am not making it up—you looked straight into my eyes, holding your gaze steadfast, and I was hooked on you forever.

Prior to your arrival, I was told by many of my contemporaries who had grandchildren, "Wait until you have a grandchild; there is nothing like it. You will love them to death!" What an awful expression, "love them to death." I wonder where that came from. I did not want to hear this. I thought, "Please do not tell me how I'm going to feel," all the time being concerned I might not be able to feel the way I am "supposed" to. Well, it was true for me, although I am sure not every grandparent feels that way; there is feeling and there is feeling. To tell you the truth, I do not give a "hoot" how other people feel. I am absolutely elated that I am capable to salivate each time I think of you. By the way, when you see me and your face lights up and you call me "Bubbe," I know you share my joy of "specialness." I'm not sure there is such a word, but it feels like a fit.

10-27-94. You slept over last night. We have to do it more

often, now that you are willing to sleep in "Uncle Johnny's bed." I could not believe how you matured, how cooperative you have become. Six months ago when you slept over, you cried when I would put you to bed and cried if I suggested you sleep in "Uncle Johnny's bed." That night you slept with us and kicked me all night. No wonder I needed to recuperate and wait until you were more mature—just like you were last night! You ate dinner with us: ravioli, cottage cheese, and peaches. You let me change your clothes into your pajamas. We watched the "Ducky" video; we had chocolate yogurt, and watched part of *Beverly Hills, 90210*. Last night, watching those steaming love scenes, I, your Bubbe, was pondering what you thought about all this commotion. What you said was, "She is crying for her daddy; she goes to sleep with daddy."

I wonder how your parents are going to restrict, or rather oversee, the programs you and your brother or brothers watch (your mom wants one more sibling for you—for herself, really—your father has perhaps other ideas) to make sure they are age appropriate. Every generation of parents goes through the same apprehensions; we all survive.

Back to last night: When I suggested going to sleep, you went willingly to Uncle Johnny's bed, asked me to lie down with you, and went to sleep in no time. In the middle of the night, you called "Bubbe" only once. I lay next to you, fell asleep with you for a while, and left you asleep until the morning.

It was good having you with me. You are my absolute joy. I am thankful for you, for the feelings you elicit in me. I am a lucky woman. I look forward to our journey.

SECTORUL I AL BEN   Extras din registrul stării civile pentru RECONSTITUIREA NAȘTERII
OFICIUL CENTRAL DE STARE CIVILĂ   PE ANUL 19 49

Nr. crt.	ANUL, LUNA ȘI ZIUA NAȘTERII	PRENUMELE ȘI SEXUL CELUI NĂSCUT	PRENUMELE NUMELE ȘI DOMICILIUL TATĂLUI ȘI AL MAMEI	EVENTUALE ÎNDREPTĂRI ÎNAINTE DE SEMNARE — SEMNĂTURI
1	2	3	4	5
81	Anul 1933 luna Octombrie ziua 10 orașul Brăila	Erica — Feminin	Emanuel gelber Fani gelber născută Türkfeld	extenta pentru a întâi...

MENȚIUNI ULTERIOARE

BIRTH CERTIFICATE

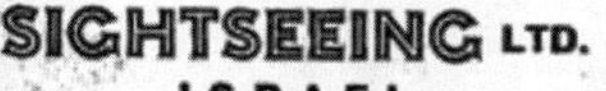

SIGHTSEEING LTD.

ISRAEL

HAIFA

4, SAFAD STREET
PHONE: 6249
CABLES: SIGHTSEE, HAIFA

ווטסיאינג בע"מ
ישראל

TEL-AVIV

81, HAYARKON STREET
PHONES: 2-1510, 2-6249
CABLES: SIGHTSEE, TEL-AVIV

TOURS THROUGHOUT ISRAEL • LUXURY SIGHTSEEING COACHES • DRIVE-YOURSELF CARS

AFFILIATED WITH ISRAEL INVESTMENTS (CANADA) LTD.

Our ref.:

Your ref.:

Subject :

Negev, 17th July 1958

M.E. Gelber,
Government Tourist Information Office,
Tel-Aviv.

Dear Sir,

 SHEIKH AWADA ABU MOUAMAR requests the pleasure of
your company on Wednesday, July 23rd 1958, at a Beduin
Dinner and "Fantasia" to be held in his encampment in the
Negev.

 Special coaches will be leaving from the office of
Sightseeing Ltd., 81 Hayarkon Street, Tel-Aviv at 4.00 p.m.

 Please confirm your participation and collect your
complimentary ticket from the office of Sightseeing Ltd.

WHILE WORKING AT THE ISRAELI GOVERNMENT TOURIST INFORMATION OFFICE,
I WAS PART OF A GROUP INVITED BY A BEDOUIN SHEIKH TO HAVE DINNER AT
HIS TENT IN THE NEGEV DESERT.

החברה הממשלתית לתיירות

GOVERNMENT TOURIST CORPORATION

TOURIST INFORMATION OFFICE

. Mendele Street 3-4 Aviv, Israel
Tel. 24266/7/8   Telex 879

לשכת המודיעין לתיירות
רחוב מנדלי 7, ת"א-ביב
טלפון 24266/7/8   מברק

15.12.58

TO WHOM IT MAY CONCERN

This is to certify that Miss. Erika Gelber
has been employed by the Government Tourist Corp.
since 3.1.57.

Miss. Gelber is on leave till 31.3.59 and is
going for a visit to Europe and the U.S.A.

Dr. W. Bloch
Director

ISRAEL Land of the Bible

LETTER FROM MY EMPLOYER IN THE ISRAELI GOVERNMENT TOURIST
INFORMATION OFFICE REGARDING MY LEAVE OF ABSENCE TO TRAVEL
TO EUROPE AND THE UNITED STATES.

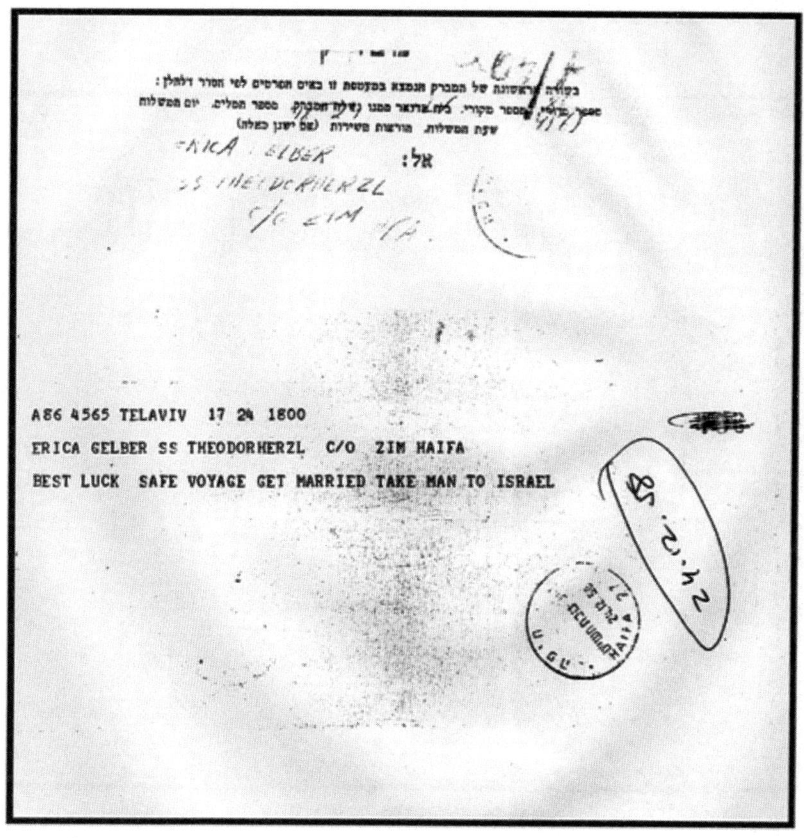

WHILE TRAVELING TO THE UNITED STATES TO VISIT MY SISTER, I RECEIVED THE FOLLOWING TELEGRAM FROM MY CO-WORKER AT THE TOURIST OFFICE, URGING ME TO BRING BACK AN AMERICAN HUSBAND.

MARRIAGE CERTIFICATE

MY UNITED STATES OF AMERICA NATURALIZATION CERTIFICATE. I BECAME AN
AMERICAN CITIZEN IN 1969.

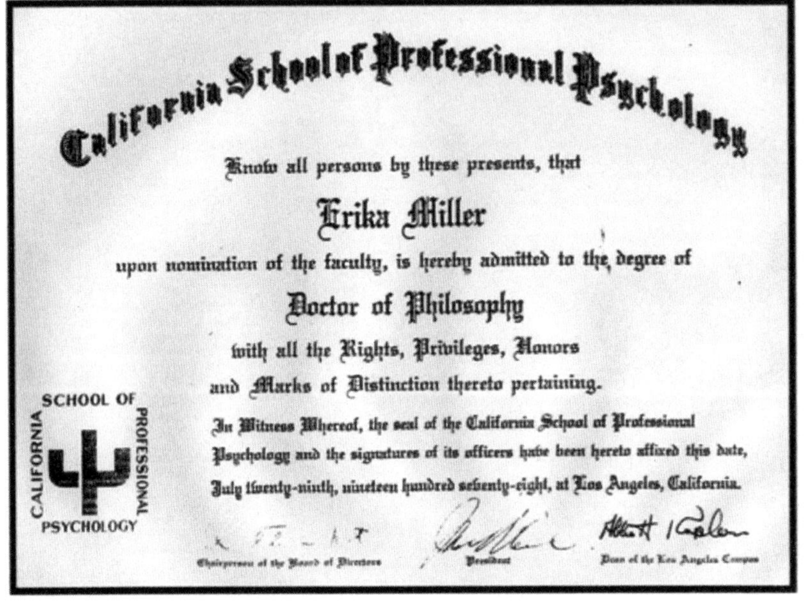

MY PHD DIPLOMA FROM THE CALIFORNIA SCHOOL OF PROFESSIONAL PSYCHOLOGY